Setting Limits
in the Classroom

▼

Setting Limits in the Classroom

How to Move Beyond the Classroom Dance of Discipline

Robert J. MacKenzie, Ed.D.

PRIMA PUBLISHING

PRIMA PUBLISHING and colophon are registered trademarks of Prima Communications, Inc.

Library of Congress Cataloging-in-Publication Data

MacKenzie, Robert J.
    Setting Limits in the Classroom / by Robert J. MacKenzie
      p.   cm.
    Includes index.
    ISBN 0-7615-0033-2
    1. Classroom management. 2. School discipline. I. Title.
LB3013.M27 1996
371.1'024—dc20   96-17629
                                                    CIP

96 97 98 99 00 HH 10 9 8 7 6 5 4 3 2 1

Printed in the United States of America

How to Order:
Single copies may be ordered from Prima Publishing, P.O. Box 1260BK, Rocklin, CA 95677; telephone (916) 632-4400. Quantity discounts are also available. On your letterhead, include information concerning the intended use of the books and the number of books you wish to purchase.

▼
_____

Contents

Contents

▼

Acknowledgments

This book began twelve years ago as a workshop for teachers titled TRIC: Training Responsible Independent Children. My sincere appreciation goes to all who participated in these workshops over the years. Your experiences, and your willingness to share them, helped refine and improve the methods in this book.

Special thanks also go to those who have supported my workshops in major ways and to those who assisted with the writing of this book.

To Bob Trigg, former superintendent of the Elk Grove Unified School District, for funding and supporting my TRIC workshops for teachers for their first ten years.

To Dave Gordon, current superintendent of the Elk Grove Unified School District, for funding and supporting my TRIC workshops for teachers during the last two years.

To the many principals of the Elk Grove Unified School District who have supported my efforts toward staff development.

To the many effective teachers I've had the privilege to observe and work with over the years. You are the real masters of effective classroom management.

To Ben Dominitz, publisher; Jennifer Basye, senior acquisitions editor; and Karen Blanco, custom publishing and promotional sales manager; and all the other good folks at Prima Publishing for believing in my project.

To Dr. Jonathon Sandoval, Professor of Education, University of California, Davis, for your technical expertise with portions of the book.

To Jean Seay for your assistance with the many charts and diagrams.

To all the parents and children I've seen over the years in my counseling work. Your successes have strengthened my beliefs in the process we shared together.

▼

Introduction

This book was written for teachers and childcare providers, but the concepts and methods it presents can be useful for anyone who wants to improve the way they communicate and set limits with children. The methods can be applied in many different settings.

Each year, teachers confront increasing numbers of children who arrive at school unprepared to follow rules, cooperate, or respect adult authority. The problem, in most cases, can be traced back to the home where the word "stop" doesn't require stopping and "no" really means yes, sometimes, or maybe.

What do children learn when limit setting is handled in this manner? They learn that following rules is optional, not required, and they carry these beliefs with them into the classroom. Worse yet, they learn to ignore the words, to challenge adult authority, and to push adults to the limit to see how far they can go.

Many parents don't realize it, but they are teaching their rules with mixed messages and making the teacher's job more difficult in the process. These mixed messages, which I refer to as "soft limits," achieve the opposite of their intended effect. They invite testing and resistance and set up adults and children for conflict. The results—behavior problems at home and in the classroom, power struggles, damaged relationships, and students poorly prepared to follow rules—take an enormous toll on children, families, our schools, and our culture.

As a family guidance counselor and parent/teacher trainer for a large Northern California school district, I see nearly two hundred students each year who are not stopping at the signals they confront in the classroom. Many are suspected of having emotional or learning problems, and a few do, but the vast majority are not suffering from any problems at all. They are simply exercising the power of their will in the hope they can wear adults down and do what they want. Often, they are successful.

By the time these students reach my office, their teachers have tried a variety of techniques to stop the misbehavior. They've tried lecturing, threatening, reasoning, explaining, bribing, cajoling, writing names on the board, taking away recesses, and making students write apology letters. They've tried making them stand in the corner, sending them to the office, issuing citations, sending home daily behavior reports, and asking their parents to spend a day time in the classroom, all without success.

Their methods range from extreme permissiveness to harsh punishment, but all these teachers share at least one thing in common: they are having trouble setting limits. They are doing the best they can with the tools they have, but the tools aren't working, and they don't know what else to do. They need effective methods.

Setting Limits in the Classroom provides you with the methods you need to stop misbehavior and teach your rules in the clearest and most understandable way. You can say good-bye to all the ineffective methods that wear you down and get you nowhere. No more reasoning, explaining, lectures, or threats. No more drawn-out consequences or exhaustive attempts at persuasion. And you can say good-bye to all the power struggles, too. Your students will know what you mean when you set clear, firm limits and support your words with effective actions. This book will show you how to do that. The methods should be a welcome alternative to the ineffective extremes of punishment and permissiveness.

In the chapters that follow, you'll learn an approach to child guidance that is clear, systematic, and developmentally appropriate for your students, one that has been tested and used successfully by thousands of teachers and parents. The methods work, and you can use them with children of all ages, from preschoolers to secondary students.

The first five chapters of this book will attempt to do what most books on guidance and discipline leave out, that is, to help you recognize the things you're doing that aren't working for you. Without this awareness, it will be difficult, if not impossible, to avoid repeating your old mistakes because most of these mistakes are made unconsciously. You'll discover your approach to limit setting, how children really learn your rules, the types of limits you're using, and the type of "classroom dance" you might be doing to get your students to cooperate.

With an understanding of what hasn't worked for you, you'll be ready to learn new skills. Chapters Six through Twelve form the core of the skill-training program. In these chapters, you'll learn how to give clear messages about your rules, stop power struggles before they begin, motivate students with encouragement, teach problem-solving skills, and support your rules with instructive consequences.

In Chapters Thirteen and Fourteen, you'll learn how to apply your new skills to solve problems with homework and help students with hyperactivity and inattention.

Learning the methods in this book will be the easiest part of your skill training. Most are fairly straightforward. For many of you, the hardest part will be to resist your temptation to revert back to old habits and do the things that haven't worked. Changing old habits is not easy.

You may recognize intellectually that the methods will lead to the type of change you desire, but the methods and the changes they bring may not feel comfortable for you or your students in the beginning. You will likely encounter pressure and resistance to change, not only from your students, but also from within yourself. Don't give up. The more you practice, the more comfortable you will feel, and the positive results will increase your confidence.

You should also expect to make mistakes and to have lapses in your consistency when you begin practicing your new skills. That's OK. Mistakes are a normal part of learning. Your goal should be improvement, and you will improve the more you practice. If you encounter unexpected problems with any of the methods, refer back to the pertinent chapters for assistance. Note the specific language used to carry out the techniques in the various examples.

Finally, many of the examples in this book reflect actual cases from my counseling and consultative work with teachers. In all cases, the names have been changed to protect the privacy of those involved.

The methods in this book have helped thousands of teachers to regain control of their classrooms and to enjoy more satisfying and cooperative relationships with students. If you are willing to invest the time and energy needed to learn the skills, you, too, can share the rewards.

Setting Limits
in the Classroom

Creating Structure That Works

Structure is the organizational foundation of the classroom. It paves the way for cooperation and learning by defining the path you want your students to stay on. In a well-structured classroom, many conflicts and behavior problems are prevented because children know what is expected. Rules, procedures, and daily routines are clear. There is less need for testing.

Because structure is so basic, many teachers overlook it and devote too little attention to it at the beginning of the year. They assume children should already know what is expected or that they will pick it up along the way. The result is more time spent on testing and disruptions and less time on teaching and learning. Everybody loses. Teachers end up exhausted as they struggle to maintain order in their classrooms and students lose valuable time for instruction.

This chapter will show you how to prevent the problems that accompany ineffective structure. You'll learn proven techniques for teaching classroom rules and procedures, defining basic student responsibilities, enlisting parent support and cooperation, and solving problems early before they get bigger. By the time you're done, you'll know how to create structure that will work for you throughout the year.

The Cost of Ineffective Structure

The lesson of structure begins the moment your students enter the classroom. There is no way to avoid it. Sooner or later—usually sooner—someone will do something he or she is not supposed to do and all the students will watch for your reaction. What you do, or fail to do, will define a rule.

Imagine, for example, that you're an eighth-grade teacher, and it's the first day of school. One of your students arrives in your first-period class wearing a headset and rocking out to one of his favorite songs. You don't like it, but you decide to ignore it. "He'll probably put it away by the time I begin teaching," you say to yourself.

He might, but what is the rule you just taught? Of course it's OK to arrive in class wearing a headset. What do you think this student and possibly others are likely to do in the future?

The issue is not whether the lesson of structure should be taught. It will be taught one way or another. The real issue is who controls the lesson—the teacher? or the students? When students control the lesson, the costs to learning and cooperation are much greater. Consider the following:

It's the first week of school in Mr. Johnson's fourth-grade class. The bell just rang, and the kids file back into class. Mr. Johnson stands at the front of the classroom and waits for the kids to settle down.

His lesson has been carefully planned and organized. He scheduled ten minutes for instructions and thirty minutes for seat work. He's ready to get started, but the kids are not. Two minutes have passed since the bell rang, and the noise level is high.

"Let's settle down a little," he says, directing his comments to several boys who are laughing and talking loudly. His words have little impact. The boys continue to laugh. Others are talking, too. Mr. Johnson waits patiently. Another minute passes.

"What's going on?" he thinks to himself. "I announced my rules the first day of class. They should know better." He tries again.

"OK, class, I'm ready to start," he says in an annoyed tone. He waits a little more. Everyone settles down except two boys.

"Craig, Terry! Are you ready to join us?" Mr. Johnson asks. The boys exchange mischievous smiles, but they stop talking for the moment. Four minutes have passed. Finally, Mr. Johnson begins his lesson.

As he gives directions for the next assignment, Mr. Johnson notices a number of students are not paying attention. "I don't want to explain this again," he says. His warning has little effect. He finishes his directions and passes out the worksheets. "You have twenty-five minutes to complete the assignment," he announces.

"I don't understand," says one student. "Yeah, what are we supposed to do?" chimes in another. Several others look confused. There isn't time for individual instructions. Mr. Johnson is frustrated.

"If you guys had been paying attention, you would know what to do," he says. "Now, listen up." He repeats the directions for the benefit of those who had not listened, eating up another five minutes. Twenty minutes left.

Finally, everyone is working. As they do, Mr. Johnson roves around the room to help those with raised hands and to intervene with disruptions. As he helps one student, he notices Craig and Terry laughing and fooling around again.

"Excuse me, Brenda," says Mr. Johnson. He approaches Craig and Terry. "Guys, would you save it for recess, please?" They smile at each other again but stop for the moment.

Mr. Johnson returns to Brenda, but by this time, other hands are in the air, and other kids are disrupting. He deals with the disruptions first, then the raised hands, and so it goes for the rest of the lesson. Hands are still in the air as the bell rings. Many don't finish.

What happened? Mr. Johnson was prepared to teach his academic lesson but not the lesson of classroom management. His class lacks structure. As a result, he spent more than a third of his time dealing with testing and disruptions.

What did his students learn? They learned the same lessons they had been learning all week. It's OK to enter the classroom noisily. Take your time to settle down. If you don't pay attention the first time, you will get a second set of directions. Worst of all, they learned that testing and disruptions are tolerated. Mr. Johnson is in for a long year. If he continues on this course, he's a good candidate for burnout.

Mistaken Beliefs About Structure

Why do some teachers like Mr. Johnson devote so little time to structure in the beginning of the year? Often the problem can be traced back to faulty beliefs about how rules should be taught and how children learn them. When it comes to teaching rules, there is certainly more disagreement than consensus. Beliefs vary regarding who should do it, how we should do it, or whether it should be done at all. Let's look at some common misconceptions that set up teachers and students for a year of testing and conflict.

1. *Teaching rules is the parents' job.*

Reality: In the classroom, teaching rules is the teacher's job, but parents can help.

What would you think if a parent called you at home one evening to complain? "I can't get Jason to clean up his room," says the frustrated parent. "He knows what he's supposed to do. Would you talk to him?"

Would you think this was a little strange?. Aren't parents supposed to be the primary authority figures in the home? Isn't it their job to enforce their rules? You might offer support and encourage them to be firm, but you recognize that the job is theirs.

The same principle applies to the classroom. In the classroom, teachers are the primary authority figures. It's their job to enforce their rules, and the kids are counting on them to do it. Parents can offer support, but the essential job belongs to the teacher. Passing responsibility to the parents won't get the job done.

2. *Children should know what I expect.*

Reality: Students need time to learn your rules and expectations.

Some teachers assume that children with any previous school experience should already know what is expected and how to behave. The assumption might hold up if all teachers were exactly alike, but this isn't the case. Their rules, expectations, and methods vary. Some are willing to overlook misbehavior, others are not. It's not realistic to expect children to understand your specific rules and expectations until they've seen you in action.

3. *I can't afford to take precious time away from instruction.*

Reality: You can't afford not to.

Pay up front and invest the necessary time in teaching your rules effectively, or do a sloppy job and pay as you go. The choice is yours, but paying as you go is more expensive.

Effective structure is one of the cheapest and least time-consuming forms of classroom management.

4. *If I cover my rules thoroughly in the beginning of the year, I shouldn't need to do it again.*

Reality: Rules need to be taught, practiced, reviewed, retaught, and practiced some more.

How many complicated lessons do you teach with full mastery in two weeks or less? Not reading, or math, or spelling, or science, or too many others. These subjects require a longer period of instruction, followed by practice, testing, review, more teaching, and more practice. When we're done, mastery is seldom 100 percent. Why should it be different with the complicated lesson of teaching classroom rules?

5. *Explaining my rules to children should be enough.*

Reality: Rules need to be taught with words and actions, not words alone.

Announcing rules during the first week of school is an important first step in the teaching-and-learning process, but words signal only our intentions. The process is incomplete. We need to support our words with effective action if we want children to regard our rules seriously. Words unsupported by action carry little weight.

6. *Children won't take me seriously unless I'm strict.*

Reality: Being strict without being respectful will not earn the willing cooperation of most students.

Children respond best when rules are communicated with firmness and respect, but firmness does not mean harshness. Fear and intimidation provide no lasting basis for cooperation.

7. *If children hear my rules often enough, the message will begin to sink in.*

Reality: Actions speak louder than words.

Imagine that you're a fifth-grade teacher. You've told your students repeatedly that it's not OK to arrive in class late from recess, but day after day the same group of kids shows up late, and nothing happens but the same old lecture. Why should they take you seriously? What would convince them that you are really serious about their prompt arrival?

Now, let's say you decide to take a different approach. The next time your students show up late, they see you standing at the door with a stopwatch. You click the watch as the last student enters and announce, "You guys owe me eight minutes—two minutes for every one that you arrived late. You'll be staying in class the first eight minutes of your next recess."

These guys really like recess. Do you think the message will get across? What convinced them—your words? or your effective action?

8. *Students resent firm rules and teachers that make them.*

Reality: Students respect teachers who establish clear, firm classroom rules, particularly when those rules are communicated in a respectful manner.

When rules are clear, firm, and carried out in a consistent and respectful manner, students know where they stand and what is expected. There is less need for testing.

9. *When my students sense that I care, they will cooperate.*

Reality: Caring is important, but caring alone is not enough to achieve consistent cooperation.

Caring and firm limits work hand in hand, but caring without firm limits will not earn you the respect of many of your strong-willed students.

10. *Male teachers make the best disciplinarians.*

Reality: In the classroom, power and authority belong to those who exercise them. Gender makes little difference.

Rules in Theory Versus Rules in Practice

Classroom rules come in two basic varieties: rules in theory and rules in practice. Each carries a different meaning and elicits a different set of responses from children. Let's look at how they work.

Rules in Theory

As the term implies, rules in theory operate at the theoretical or hypothetical level. They are words that represent your hopes and expectations for how students should behave. How do they work? Usually they are announced, but they may take the form of requests or directives.

Many teachers regard their announced rules to be their actual rules. In reality, the two may be different depending on what happens after the talking is over. For example, consider how the following three teachers communicate their rules in theory. Later we'll examine the rules they actually practice.

Mrs. Atkins and the Morning Circle It's time for morning circle, a daily sharing activity in Mrs. Atkins's preschool class. The kids are all seated on the carpet near the blackboard. As the activity begins, Matthew, age four, presses his foot against the back of the girl in front of him and pulls on her sweater.

"Matthew, we don't put our hands or feet on others when we're in morning circle," says Mrs. Atkins. "We sit like this." She models the behavior she wants by sitting Indian style with her hands in her lap. Matthew decides to cooperate for the moment.

Mr. Larson and the Toys in Class Mr. Larson, a fifth-grade teacher, notices that some of his students have been bringing small toys or trading cards to class and playing with them during instruction. He decides to put a stop to it.

"If you bring toys or cards to school, you need to keep them in your desk or backpack," he says. "If you have them out during class, I will take them away and return them to your parents at our next teacher-parent conference."

Miss Stallings and Her Tardy Students Miss Stallings, an eleventh-grade government teacher, is concerned about the number of students who have been arriving late for class. She decides to bring it up with her students.

"Class, I expect you to be in the door before the fifth-period bell rings," begins Miss Stallings. "If you don't, you will be tardy, and you will have to go to the attendance office to pick up a tardy slip before you can come back to class. If you get three tardies in any one semester, you'll have to spend two hours after school in the silent study center."

Rules in Practice

Rules in practice are defined by your actions or what your students actually experience after all the talking is over. The behavior you're willing to tolerate defines your actual classroom standards.

How do students know your rules in practice? They test, then watch what you do. Your actions will clarify what you really expect. Now, let's return to our three earlier examples and see what happened when the students decided to test.

Mrs. Atkins and the Morning Circle Several minutes after Matthew was asked to stop putting his hands and feet on others, he decides to test. He gives Sara another nudge with his foot and tugs the back of her sweater.

"Matthew," says Mrs. Atkins, "you need to sit by yourself for the rest of circle time." She gets out a carpet strip and sets it down about five feet away from the others.

Did Matthew's teacher practice the rule she announced? You bet. She said stop, and that's what Matthew

9

experienced when he decided to test. Her message was clear, and so was her rule. She may need to repeat this lesson several times before Matthew is convinced, but if she does, Matthew will surely get the message.

Mr. Larson and the Toys in Class Later in the afternoon, after Mr. Larson announced his rule about playing with toys in class, he notices one of his students passing her troll doll to another girl in her table group.

"Sandy, what did I say about playing with toys in class?" he asks. "Now put it away, please." He lets it pass with just a warning. The lesson isn't lost on others.

The next day, he catches Dale and Patrick playing with baseball cards. "Guys, do you want to lose them?" Mr. Larson asks. "If not, put them away." Again, he lets it pass with just a warning.

Before the week is over, there are several more incidents and several more warnings. In one case, he actually confiscates some cards but returns them after school with instructions not to bring them back.

What is the rule Mr. Larson actually practices? Of course it's OK to play with toys in class. All you get is warnings. Why should anyone take Mr. Larson's rule very seriously?

Miss Stallings and Her Tardy Students The day following Miss Stallings's announcement, three students arrive late for class. She greets them at the door.

"You need to go to the attendance office to get tardy slips," she says.

"Oh, come on, Miss Stallings," pleads one girl. "We had to go back to our lockers to get our leadership reports. We won't do it again."

"Well, the reason is related to class," Miss Stallings says to herself. "Maybe I should give them a break."

"OK, I'll let it go this time," says Miss Stallings, "but next time you'll have to get a tardy slip."

The lesson isn't lost on others. There are more late arrivals that week, and each time, the students have good excuses. The pattern continues into the second and third weeks. At the end of the third week, only one student has actually been sent for a tardy slip. He showed up more than five minutes late and couldn't come up with a good excuse.

What's the rule in practice here? Sure, it's OK to show up late for class as long as you can come up with a good excuse. That's what the students learned, and that's what they will probably continue to do. They have little cause to regard Miss Stallings's spoken rule very seriously.

Introducing Rules to Students

We can help students learn our rules and get off to a good start at the beginning of the year by teaching our rules as systematically as we would any other subject, from the first day they enter our classroom. The following tips will help you get started during the critical first four weeks of the semester.

On the First Day

- Introduce your general rules or rules in theory. Keep them broad and inclusive and avoid extensive lists. Many teachers find the three following rules to be sufficient:

  1. Cooperate with your teacher and classmates.

  2. Respect the rights and property of others.

  3. Carry out your student responsibilities.

- Post your general classroom rules in a visible area for elementary and secondary students.

11

- Describe your classroom procedures such as how students should enter the room, get ready for lunch, or prepare to leave at the end of the day.
- Describe the guidance procedures you use when classroom rules are tested or violated.
- Be prepared to use your guidance procedures the first time testing occurs. The lesson won't be missed by others.
- Announce that you will send home a list of your classroom rules and guidance procedures.

During the First Two Weeks

- Review your general classroom rules daily as well as any specific rules that have been tested or violated. Ask questions to be sure students understand what you expect.
- Set aside time each day to teach classroom routines and procedures. Select a different procedure to work on each day or devote more time to procedures that present problems such as sitting in morning circle, lining up for recess, or going to time-out.

  Keep the lessons simple and concrete, particularly with preschool and elementary-school students. Don't assume that your words will be enough to convey your message. Show them what you mean by modeling the correct behavior. Walk them through hypothetical situations to make sure they understand what you expect. Continue practicing the lesson until they get it right.

- Expect testing and be prepared to follow through. There is only so much you can teach with verbal instruction, practice, and review. Most of your students will be convinced you mean business when they see how much time and energy you're willing to devote to teaching your rules. They will accept your rules as stated and do their best to follow them.

Some students will have to experience your rules in practice many times before they will be convinced. These lessons won't be planned or scheduled. They might take place at any time during the day. When they do, you will need to follow through and support your rule with effective action.

During the First Month

• Continue teaching your rules and procedures.

• Expect testing and be prepared to follow through. The heaviest testing usually occurs during the first four to six weeks of school. Be prepared to support your rules with effective action. Your consistency will buy huge credibility points for later on.

• Schedule preventive parent conferences for students who test excessively during the first four weeks. You'll need parent support and cooperation.

Throughout the Year

• Review classroom rules and procedures periodically.

• Continue to follow through with effective action. Learning to follow rules is an ongoing process.

• Involve parents and develop a home/school guidance plan when efforts to resolve problems individually with a student do not lead to improvement.

Defining Basic Student Responsibilities

One of the most important lessons children learn in school is the lesson of good work habits or how to be responsible for completing a task. Children who learn good work habits become not only successful students but successful people. Good work habits and success go hand in hand.

How do students acquire good work habits? They acquire work habits the same way they acquire other skills—through a teaching-and-learning process. They need direction, practice, corrective feedback, and opportunities to experience the consequences of their efforts, both positive and negative.

Teachers can help the process along by being clear about their expectations, by acknowledging and rewarding compliance, and by holding students accountable when they do less than their part. The following suggestions should help.

On the First Day

- Share your expectations for basic student responsibilities. Keep your list brief. A sample list might be:

  1. Keep track of your own books and assignments.

  2. Start your work on time and allow enough time to finish.

  3. Ask for help when you need it.

  4. Do your own work.

  5. Turn your work in on time.

  6. Accept responsibility for grades or other consequences.

- Post a list of basic student responsibilities in a visible area in the classroom.

- Share your expectations for homework and describe homework procedures. Be clear about when assignments are given, when assignments are due, and what happens when work is not completed.

14

- Introduce your accountability procedures and explain how they work.

During the First Week

- Review your list of basic responsibilities daily.
- Review your accountability procedures daily.
- Inform your students that you will send home a list of their basic responsibilities, your homework policy, and a description of your accountability procedures so their parents know what is expected.
- Send home a work folder each Friday for parents to sign, make comments, and return with their child on Monday.

Throughout the Year

- Review your list of basic student responsibilities as needed.
- Follow through with accountability procedures.
- Schedule conferences with parents of students who are consistently noncompliant with homework. Discuss your concerns and encourage them to implement the corrective steps described in chapter 14.

Accountability Procedures

The lesson of responsibility is difficult to teach without accountability. Your students need to know from the beginning that they are expected to do their part and that there will be consequences, positive and negative, associated with their performance. The following procedures help teach responsibility by holding children accountable for their work.

Fun Friday

Fun Friday is a clever procedure used by elementary teachers to acknowledge and reward good work habits. Students become eligible for Fun Friday after they have completed all assigned work for the week. A block of time is set aside on Friday afternoons for preferred activities students can do quietly at their seats. The list of activities is usually decided in advance by the teacher and students, and the activities are selected from a cabinet or shelf in the classroom. Students who are not eligible use the time instead to catch up on incomplete work.

Friday Work Folders

Friday work folders are a simple and effective method for helping parents stay up-to-date on their child's progress. The procedure is easy to carry out. Each Friday, the teacher sends home a packet of all the work the student has complete and turned in for that week. Attached to the packet is a form indicating whether all items were completed and which items remain incomplete (Figure 1A). The parents review the packet, sign and date an entry on the inside cover of the folder, and make any comments if they desire.

Friday work folders have many advantages. They allow parents to closely monitor the quality of their child's work and compliance with homework and in-class assignments. They provide an ongoing communication channel between school and home, and they serve as an early detection system so parents and teachers can deal with student problems early before they develop into more serious problems.

Makeup Sessions for Missed Work

This accountability procedure has been a fixture in public-school education for generations. The system is very simple.

**Figure IA. Sample feedback sheet
for Friday work folders**

Name _____   Week _____

_____ Great week! All work completed.
_____ Work is not complete. Please finish the fol-
      lowing by Monday.

When children dawdle, avoid, procrastinate, or otherwise fail to complete assigned work during class time, they are required to make up that work during recess. In effect, the loss of recess time becomes the logical consequence for not completing their work. The procedure is not recommended for students who fail to complete work on time because they lack skills.

Enlisting Parent Support and Cooperation

The focus thus far has been on helping students get acquainted with our structure. We've examined various methods to introduce rules, teach class procedures, and define basic responsibilities. The final step in creating a structure that works is to involve the parents in the process. Our structure will not be complete until home and school operate under the same set of rules and expectations.

How do we enlist parental support? There is no one right way, but there are some guidelines we should follow. First, be proactive. Contact parents early before problems develop. Second, give parents all the information they require to back you up. It is not enough to simply expect their support. Provide them with the information they require to be supportive.

What's the alternative if we don't make early contact or provide parents with the information they need? How will they know what we expect or how to support us? The chances are they won't know, not until we need their help due to a problem that has developed with their child. How are they likely to feel if we seek their support under these circumstances?—defensive? angry? embarrassed? Sure. Is this any way to begin a cooperative relationship?

Some teachers wait until their first set of teacher-parent conferences to share the information parents need. This practice has several disadvantages. What parents like to hear at their first conference that their child has been misbehaving or not completing work for the last eight to ten weeks? When we allow problems to develop into patterns, we don't inspire parent confidence in our classroom management skills. Teachers who wait too long to contact parents risk turning a potential supporter into an adversary.

The choices are clear: Either we share our rules and expectations early and start off on a positive note, or we keep parents in the dark and risk alienating them when the focus of our first contact is a problem with their child. The following recommendations should help you get off to a positive start with parents.

During the First Week

- Send parents a letter describing your general classroom rules, guidance procedures, list of student responsibilities, homework policy, and suggestions for how they can support you at home. Ask parents to review the information with their child (Figures 1B, 1C, 1D, and 1E).

Figure 1B. Sample parent notification letter

Teacher's name _____

Student's name _____

Dear Parents,

   We're off to a good start. I'm enjoying getting
to know your child and look forward to meeting you
personally during our back-to-school night next
week. I'm sure you are as committed as I am to
seeing that your child gets off to a good start.
For that reason, I am sending a copy of my classroom rules, a list of basic student responsibilities, my homework policy, and a description of
some of the procedures I use to keep you informed.

   When problems arise in the classroom, I will
make a complete effort to resolve the matter individually with the student. If we are unable to resolve the problem, then I often ask parents for
support and assistance. Together we can usually
resolve problems early and get students pointed in
the right direction.

   Please support me by reviewing the attached
lists of classroom rules, student responsibilities, and homework policy with your child, and indicate a telephone number where you can be reached
during school hours. Thanks for your support. I
look forward to a great year.

Parent phone number during school hours _____

Figure IC. Classroom rules

Classroom Rules

- Cooperate with your teacher and classmates.

- Respect the rights and property of others.

- Carry out your basic student responsibilities.

Figure ID. Basic student responsibilities

Basic Student Responsibilities

- Keep track of your ˊown books and assignments.

- Start your work on time and allow time to finish.

- Ask for help when you need it.

- Do your own work.

- Turn your work in on time.

- Accept responsibility for grades and other
  consequences.

Figure 1E. Homework policy and Friday folder procedure

Homework Policy and Friday Folder Procedure

Each week, homework assignments will be sent home with the student on Monday and are due by Friday for full credit. All completed work will be sent home on Friday in your child's Friday work folder. Please review the folder, sign it, make any comments you desire, and return the folder with your child on Monday.

Students who have completed all assigned work for the week by Friday morning are eligible for participation in Fun Friday, a preferred activity period on Friday afternoons. Students who are not eligible will use that time to catch up on remaining work.

Any work that is not completed on Friday will be noted in the student's Friday folder. It is the student's responsibility to complete that work over the weekend and return it in his or her folder on Monday for partial credit.

During the First Month

- Schedule a back-to-school night during the first two to three weeks of school. Back-to-school nights are an efficient way to share a lot of information with a large number of people and still provide opportunities for questions and input. Teachers can accomplish in one hour what would take many hours over a period of weeks to accomplish by phone. Topics to be covered during the meeting should include:

1. Skills students will learn during the year

2. Classroom rules

3. Guidance procedures

4. Basic student responsibilities

5. Homework policy

6. Friday folder system

7. Specific steps parents can take at home to support you

Be prepared to provide extra copies of the materials you sent home during the first week for parents who may have lost or misplaced them. Set aside time at the end for questions, comments, or input. A well-run conference will inspire parent confidence and trust that you run an effective, well-organized classroom.

- Make phone contact with parents who did not attend your back-to-school night. Try to limit your call to ten to fifteen minutes and cover the following:

1. Share a positive incident or observation that characterizes their child.

2. Ask if they have any questions about the materials you sent home during the first week.

3. Encourage them to review the information with their child.

4. Express your appreciation for their support.

5. Schedule parent conferences when students persistently test limits, violate classroom rules, or fail to carry out their basic responsibilities. Early intervention is the key to gaining parental support and cooperation.

Chapter Summary

Effective structure is one of the easiest, least expensive, and least time-consuming forms of classroom management, but many teachers overlook the importance of structure in the beginning of the year. They assume that children should already know what is expected or that they will pick it up along the way—a costly assumption that sets up both teacher and students for a year of testing and conflict.

The lesson of structure will be taught one way or another. There is no way to avoid it. The real issue is who controls the lesson. When students control the lesson, the cost to cooperation and learning are much greater. Time that should be spent in instruction is spent instead handling testing, disruptions, and damage control.

The choices are clear. Either we begin early and invest the time required to teach our rules and enlist parent support, or we exhaust ourselves trying to accomplish these tasks as we go and risk alienating parents in the process. Prevention is always the better way to go. Creating structure early in the year leads to smoother sailing later on.

▼
Chapter

2

How Teachers Teach Their Rules

Years ago, when I first began giving workshops, I didn't ask the participants what methods they already used, nor did I spend any time discussing different training models. I just assumed we were operating with a common understanding about what works best, and I jumped in during the first session and shared the methods I knew would be effective. As it turned out, this mistake led me to an important discovery.

After my first few workshops, I began receiving thank-you notes with appreciative comments that really concerned me. "Thanks for helping me become firm with my limits," one teacher said. "I don't nag them all day like I used to. Now I only ask them two or three times, then I give them choices." Another teacher commented, "Limited choices work great. When my students dawdle, I give them a choice—you can finish on time or lose your recesses for a week. They usually finish up."

I became particularly concerned when one fifth-grade teacher told me how much he liked logical consequences. "When my students are disrespectful to me, I make them stay in during recess and write me an apology letter. Then I make them read it to me in front of the class."

"Was this one of my workshops?" I wondered. How is it possible that someone could so misinterpret the methods I was sharing? But the comments continued, and to my dismay, parents were doing the same thing in my parenting workshops.

Then it occurred to me what was happening. We all thought we shared a common understanding, but we were viewing the methods from very different perspectives. Those who believed in punishment used them punitively, and those who believed in permissiveness used them permissively. They all thought they were doing things differently, but they were simply repeating their old mistakes with new methods. I could see this was not a conscious process.

When I give workshops today, my first task is to help the participants become acquainted with their current guidance approach so they can recognize and avoid their old mistakes. I usually begin by demonstrating how a typical discipline problem can be handled in three different ways: punitively, permissively, or democratically. Then we examine the teaching and learning process that accompanies each approach. Most teachers find this helpful. They recognize their approach by examining the methods used by others.

Let's look at how three teachers handle a typical playground problem—rough play. Each uses a different guidance approach.

It's morning recess. A group of boys divides up into teams to play a karate commando game. The teams hide, sneak up on each other, then hold mock battles. It's the last part that leads to problems. Several students have been hurt. The game has been banned from the playground, but some students try to play it anyway.

The mock battle is under way when Mrs. Fisher, the yard-duty teacher, notices what's going on. She watches with concern. The boys see her, too, but the game continues with more flying kicks and punches that barely miss.

Finally, one boy is grazed by a kick. He holds his side and grimaces. Mrs. Fisher intervenes. "Guys, that game doesn't look safe," she says. "I'm afraid someone is going to get hurt. Kicks can cause serious injuries. That's why we don't allow that game."

"We're just pretending," says one student. "We'll be careful."

"I know you will, but what you're doing worries me. I really wish you would stop," she says. They do, as long as Mrs. Fisher is in the area, but as soon as she leaves, the battle resumes.

Next recess, Mr. Howard is on yard duty. When he sees the boys playing the karate game, he rushes to the scene. "Stop!" he shouts. "Are you guys playing that karate game again?"

"No, we were just fooling around," says one student.

"Don't lie to me, young man, or you'll find yourself in even more trouble," warns Mr. Howard. He points an accusing finger at the boy and gives him a stern, intimidating look. "Now tell me who all was involved here?"

Mr. Howard spends the next ten minutes interrogating the group. He listens to their pleas of innocence or guilt and threatens further consequences if he discovers anyone lying. Finally he's satisfied he has the culprits. He writes up five citations and sends the offenders to the office. "I hope this helps you remember the rules next time you decide to play that game," he adds.

The boys are angry and set on revenge. As they reach the edge of the playground, they get off some parting shots. "You're a great teacher all right," shouts one student sarcastically. "A great jerk is more like it," adds another. They all laugh.

"Keep it up, guys!" shouts Mr. Howard. "The principal will hear about this, too. You're just adding to your punishment."

A few days later, it's Mrs. Taylor's turn to supervise recess. When she sees what appears to be the beginning of a mock karate battle, she approaches the group. "Guys, you'll have to choose another game to play," she says in a matter-of-fact tone. "That game is not allowed. If you play it again, you'll have to sit out the rest of the recess on the bench. Thanks for cooperating."

No lectures. No pleading. No threats or accusations. She simply gives them the information they need to make an acceptable choice. Sure, there was some grumbling. The boys weren't happy about it. A few were probably tempted to test, but nobody wanted to spend their recess on the bench. Cooperation was the best choice.

Each teacher in the previous examples was trying to teach a rule about acceptable playground behavior, but only one enjoyed much success. Mrs. Fisher used the permissive approach. Her methods were respectful but not very firm. The boys ignored her and did what they wanted.

Mr. Howard used the punitive or autocratic approach. His methods were firm but not very respectful. The boys rebelled.

Mrs. Taylor used the democratic approach. Her methods were firm and respectful. She gave the boys the information they needed to make an acceptable choice, and they cooperated.

Do you think the three teachers in my example would show similar inconsistency if they were teaching a lesson in reading, math, or spelling? Not likely. Why then is there so much inconsistency when it comes to teaching rules?

Actually, the teachers in my example are no further apart in their training methods than the rest of us. The methods they use simply reflect the range of practices in our culture at large. We're all over the map. Some believe in permissveness. Others take a punitive or autocratic view. Some are democratic, and still others flip-flop back and forth between the extremes of permissiveness and punishment.

Most of us teach our rules from one or more of these basic training models. Each model is premised on a different set of beliefs about how children learn, the teacher's role in the training process, and the proper distribution of power and responsibility between adults and children. Each model teaches a different set of lessons about cooperation, responsibility, and your expectations for acceptable behavior. Let's take a closer look now at each of these models.

The Permissive Approach (Respectful but Not Firm)

Permissiveness emerged prominently in the 1960s and 1970s as a reaction against the rigidity and autocratic nature of the punitive approach. Many parents and teachers were looking for a new and more democratic approach to raising children based on principles of freedom, equality, and mutual respect.

Putting these principles into practice, however, was not as easy as it sounded. This was uncharted territory for those of us who grew up with the punitive model. How do you do it? Was it a simple matter of relaxing our rules and expectations and giving children more freedom and control? That's what many tried. They experimented with open classrooms, relaxed structure, more freedom, and choices at home and in school. But the experiment often backfired because a vital ingredient was left out—limits.

Freedom without limits is not democracy. It's anarchy, and children trained with anarchy do not learn respect for rules or authority or how to handle their freedom responsibly. They think primarily of themselves and develop an exaggerated sense of their own power and control. The examples of a failed experiment are all around us.

Let's look at how one teacher uses the permissive approach to handle a typical classroom problem—disruption.

Mrs. Weaver, a sixth-grade teacher, passes out worksheets for the next assignment and tells the class they have twenty minutes to finish up before lunch. The students begin working quietly at their seats.

After a few minutes, Mrs. Weaver hears Nate talking to a girl in his table group. He talks softly at first, so Mrs. Weaver ignores it, but his talking continues and the volume increases. She decides to intervene.

"Nate, don't you think it's getting a little loud in here?" she says. "Others are trying to work."

He settles down for a while, but within a few minutes, he talks to someone else, softly at first, then louder.

"Nate, you have fifteen minutes to finish up before lunch," reminds Mrs. Weaver. "You need to do a little less talking and a little more working, OK?"

Five minutes go by before Nate disrupts again. This time, he laughs and jokes with another boy. Mrs. Weaver feels annoyed. She walks over and looks at him impatiently. "How many times do I have to ask you?" she asks.

"I wasn't too loud," argues Nate.

"Well, you sounded too loud to me," replies Mrs. Weaver. "Besides, what you're doing isn't respectful to me or your classmates, and I don't appreciate it. If you don't stop talking, I'm going to move you from your table group. I'm not going to ask you again."

Nate returns to his work, briefly, but within a few minutes, he talks again. Mrs. Weaver intervenes.

"I've had enough of this, Nate!" says a frustrated Mrs. Weaver. "Move your desk away from your group." She points to an area about six feet away.

"But Mrs. Weaver, that's not fair!" protests Nate. "I was asking Tim for some help. I wasn't bothering anybody."

"You were distracting Tim from his work," counters Mrs. Weaver. "What are you supposed to do when you need help?"

"Raise my hand," says Nate.

"Right!" replies Mrs. Weaver, "and I hope you remember it. This time, it's a warning. If I hear any more talking, I will move you. I really mean it." Nate settles down once again.

What did Nate experience? It wasn't cooperating, at least not for very long. Instead, he experienced a lot of words and very little action. Based on his experience, he has little cause to regard Mrs. Weaver's rule about disrupting very seriously.

Permissive teachers are constantly shifting gears and trying different verbal tactics to convince their students to cooperate. They do a lot of repeating, reminding, warning, offering second chances, pleading, cajoling, bargaining, bribing, arguing, debating, reasoning, lecturing, and trying other forms of verbal persuasion. Consequences, if they are used at all, are typically late and ineffective. By the time everything is said and done, teachers usually end up compromising away their rules or giving in altogether. Often children end up getting their own way. Permissiveness is humiliating to teachers.

As a training approach, permissiveness is much worse than punishment for both adults and children. It doesn't accomplish any of our basic training goals. It doesn't stop misbehavior. It doesn't teach responsibility, and it doesn't teach our intended lessons about rules or authority. Permissiveness does not provide children with the information they need to make acceptable choices about their behavior.

What do children learn from permissiveness? They learn to ignore our words and push us to the point of action to clarify what we really expect. They become very skillful at ignoring, tuning out, resisting, avoiding, arguing, debating, bargaining, challenging, and defying. They don't do it maliciously. They simply do it because it works. Their experiences have taught them that "Rules are for others, not me. I make my own rules, and I do what I want."

Let's take a closer look at what happened between Nate and his teacher by examining a diagram of their interaction. We'll place Mrs. Weaver's behavior on the left side of the diagram and Nate's behavior on the right. Visual diagrams often reveal, better than words, the various steps in an interactional sequence (Figure 2A).

The first thing you probably notice is the length of this diagram. Permissive teachers use a lot of different tactics. Mrs. Weaver is no exception. She begins at point A by attempting to ignore the misbehavior, a strategy that seldom works. Nate continues talking. When his volume increases, she attempts to give him a signal. She asks him if the noise level is too high and points out that others are working quietly.

Did you hear a clear message that Nate should stop talking? Neither did Nate. He continues talking a short time later. So Mrs. Weaver tries a different tactic. She points out how little time he has to complete his assignment and asks him to do a little less talking.

What is a little less talking? Does that mean some is OK? How much then? And how will Nate know? Of course, he'll have to test, and that's exactly what he does. He continues talking.

So Mrs. Weaver switches gears again. She tries repeating and reminding. Does this work? No. Nate tries to hook her into an argument. It works.

She takes the bait and argues with him about the volume of his talking, but now the argument is a source of disruption. She lectures him briefly about respect then threatens to move him away from his table group if he disrupts again. Is Nate persuaded by the lecture or threat?

Figure 2A. Diagram of a permissive interaction

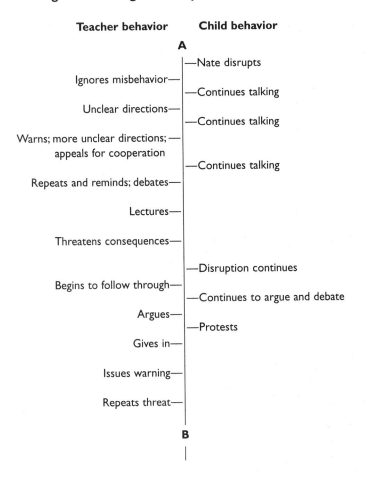

Teacher behavior | Child behavior

A

Ignores misbehavior— —Nate disrupts

—Continues talking

Unclear directions— —Continues talking

Warns; more unclear directions; appeals for cooperation— —Continues talking

Repeats and reminds; debates—

Lectures—

Threatens consequences—

—Disruption continues

Begins to follow through— —Continues to argue and debate

Argues— —Protests

Gives in—

Issues warning—

Repeats threat—

B

Not a chance. He thinks she's bluffing, so he calls her on it. He continues testing.

With her credibility on the line, Mrs. Weaver finally decides to act. She tells Nate to move. It looks as though she might actually follow through, too, but Nate skillfully hooks her into another round of arguments and debates. She listens, tries to be fair, and decides to let the incident pass with just a warning. The encounter ends at point B with Mrs. Weaver repeating her threat to move Nate if he continues talking.

Why didn't Nate cooperate? The reason is simple. He didn't have to. Cooperation was optional, not required. Mrs. Weaver was unwilling to support her words with effective action (consequences). She relied instead on persuasion to get her message across.

Can you imagine what things would be like if our traffic laws were enforced in this way? Visualize yourself driving home. The traffic is light, and each time you approach an intersection, you run the stoplight. Eventually, a cop sees you and pulls you over.

"You ran three stoplights," he says. "That's against the law, and our laws are there for your safety and protection. If everyone disregarded stoplights, we would have a lot of serious accidents. I would appreciate it if you would please try to follow the law in the future." Then he gets back in his car and drives off, and that's all that ever happens. Would this stop you from running stoplights in the future? Do you think this approach would serve as a deterrent to others?

Permissive teachers are a lot like the cop in my example. They give lots of warnings, reminders, second chances, and persuasive reasons why kids should stop at their stop signals. They may threaten to write tickets, and sometimes they actually do, but most of the time kids talk their way out of it and things pass with just a warning. Without tickets (consequences) to hold them accountable, kids have little cause to regard their teacher's rules seriously.

Why are permissive teachers reluctant to use consequences to enforce their rules? Most have the best of intentions. They don't mean to be vague. They're trying to be respectful, but they don't know how to be firm and respectful at the same time. Permissive teachers are afraid that the temporary frustration that accompanies consequences might damage children psychologically.

Let's do a little reality testing with this assumption. Are you accustomed to always getting your own way out in the world? When you don't, do you feel good about it? Aren't we supposed to feel frustrated when we don't get what we want? Isn't that how we learn to adjust to reality? When we prevent children from experiencing the consequences of their behavior, we also prevent much of their learning.

If permissive teachers are reluctant to use consequences to enforce their rules, how do they think they can stop misbehavior? Permissive teachers believe children will stop misbehaving when children realize that stopping is the right thing to do. The teacher's job, therefore, is to convince them to accept this belief.

The belief might hold up if all children were born with compliant temperaments. Compliant children are eager to please. Most will cooperate because that's the right thing to do. But what about strong-willed children or children who fall somewhere in between? Often the only reason they cooperate is because they have to.

Do you recall our earlier example about the boys and the karate game? Why did they finally stop playing that dangerous game? Was it because stopping was the right thing to do? No, they stopped because they had to. They didn't want to experience the consequence that accompanied the choice to continue. They finally got a clear message about what was expected.

When our words are supported by effective action, children receive a clear signal about our rules and expectations. They understand that our spoken rules are the rules we practice and learn to take our words seriously. When our words are not supported by effective action, however, many children will ignore our words and continue to do what they want. The message they receive comes across like this: "I don't like what you're doing, but I'm not going to make you stop, at least not for a while."

How do kids know when they really are expected to stop? Often, they don't. The only way they will know is by testing our limits to see how far they can go. That's what permissiveness teaches them to do (Figure 2B).

Figure 2B. The permissive approach

Teacher's beliefs	Children will cooperate when they understand that cooperation is the right thing to do.
	My job is to serve my children and keep them happy.
	Consequences that upset my children cannot be effective.
Power and control	All for children.
Problem-solving process	Problem solving by persuasion.
	Win-lose (children win).
	Teachers do most of the problem solving.
What children learn	"Rules are for others, not me. I do as I wish."
	Teachers serve children.
	Teachers are responsible for solving children's problems.
	Dependency, disrespect, self-centeredness.
How children respond	Testing limits.
	Challenging and defying rules and authority.
	Ignoring and tuning out words.
	Wearing teachers down with words.

The Punitive Approach (Firm but Not Respectful)

The punitive or autocratic approach has been a stable fixture in American schools for a long time. It was the dominant training system prior to the 1960s and remains one of the most widely used training models. Its trademark has been its predictability. Children respond to coercion and punishment the same way today that they did fifty or more years ago.

Teachers who rely on the punitive or autocratic approach often find themselves in the roles of detective, judge, jailer, and probation officer. Their job is to investigate children's misdeeds, determine guilt, assign blame, impose penalties, and carry out sentences. Teachers direct and control the problem-solving process, which is often adversarial. Penalties tend to be drawn out and severe. Let's look at how one teacher uses this approach to handle a problem with disruption.

Mr. Stover, a fourth-grade teacher, is writing instructions on the blackboard when he hears giggling at the back of the room. Several students look at Jason who does his best to appear innocent. Mr. Stover isn't convinced.

"OK guys, what's going on?" asks Mr. Stover in an annoyed tone. "What's so funny?"

"He made us laugh," says one student, pointing to Jason. Jason shrugs his shoulders. Mr. Stover gives him a stern, disapproving look, then returns to his work on the blackboard.

A few minutes pass, then more giggles, only louder this time. When Mr. Stover turns, he sees Jason making mocking hand gestures to the amusement of his classmates. "That's enough Jason!" says Mr. Stover angrily.

"I wasn't doing anything," replies Jason, believing he wasn't observed.

"Don't lie to me," says Mr. Stover. "I saw what you were doing, and I don't appreciate it. I expect that kind of behavior from a first grader but not from you. Keep it up and you're going to find yourself in big trouble." He gives Jason another stern, intimidating look.

A few minutes pass, then Jason makes an even bolder move. When Mr. Stover's back is turned, Jason stands up and shakes his finger in a mock punitive gesture. The giggles turn into laughter. Mr. Stover intervenes again.

"What does it take to get through to you, Jason?" asks Mr. Stover. "Do you enjoy making a fool of yourself?"

"Do you enjoy being such a boring teacher?" counters Jason.

"That's enough!" shouts Mr. Stover, his face flushed with anger. "You've gone too far. Take your chair out in the hallway and write one hundred times I will not be disrespectful to my teacher."

Jason spends the next twenty minutes in the hallway. When the bell rings for recess, he tries to join his classmates. Mr. Stover intercepts him.

"Not so fast, Jason," says Mr. Stover. "Where are the sentences?"

"I didn't write them," says Jason defiantly, "and you can't make me."

"You won't go out to recess until you do," says Mr. Stover.

"Oh yeah? See what I care," says Jason. He would rather sit out the recess than give Mr. Stover the satisfaction of thinking he won.

Sure, Mr. Stover did get his message across, eventually, but what did he really accomplish? Did Jason leave the encounter with increased respect for Mr. Stover's rules or authority? Did Jason receive an instructive lesson in cooperation or responsibility? No. Jason learned what he experienced—a lesson in hurtful problem solving.

As a training model, the punitive approach has many limitations and only partially accomplishes our basic training goals. It usually does stop unwanted behavior in an immediate situation, but it doesn't teach independent problem solving, and it doesn't teach positive lessons about responsibility or self-control. Why? Because teachers make all the decisions, and teachers do all the problem solving. Teachers exercise all of the power and control, and kids are left out of the process. In effect, the punitive approach takes responsibility and learning opportunities away from children.

Let's take a closer look at the methods Mr. Stover used by examining a diagram of their interaction (Figure 2C).

At point A, Mr. Stover notices the disruption and intervenes with some quick detective work. His tone is angry and adversarial. The focus is on right and wrong, guilt and blame, good guys and bad guys. The kids pick up on the dynamics quickly. They deny their guilt and attempt to place the blame on each other. The game of cops and robbers is under way, but so far the robbers are winning. Mr. Stover's detective work leads nowhere. So he tries intimidation.

Now the students know he is hooked. Their disruption continues, but Mr. Stover gets his evidence. He catches Jason in the act. When Jason denies his guilt, Mr. Stover accuses him of lying and confronts him with the vidence.

At this point, Mr. Stover's anger and frustration take over. He has completely personalized the conflict, and he is determined to make Jason pay for his crimes. The issue of disruption is now secondary to the hurtful and escalating power struggle that dominates the interaction. Mr. Stover begins by shaming and blaming Jason in front of the class, then he adds a challenge. He tells Jason to "keep it up" and threatens further consequences if he does.

Figure 2C. Diagram of a punitive interaction

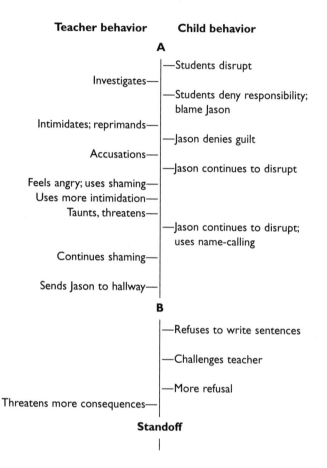

Teacher behavior   **Child behavior**

A

—Students disrupt

Investigates—

—Students deny responsibility;
 blame Jason

Intimidates; reprimands—

—Jason denies guilt

Accusations—

—Jason continues to disrupt

Feels angry; uses shaming—
Uses more intimidation—
Taunts, threatens—

—Jason continues to disrupt;
 uses name-calling

Continues shaming—

Sends Jason to hallway—

B

—Refuses to write sentences

—Challenges teacher

—More refusal

Threatens more consequences—

Standoff

Isn't this like waving a red cape in front of an angry bull? What would you predict? Right, the strategy backfires. Jason feels humiliated and retaliates with further disruption and name-calling. Mr. Stover responds on the same level. The drama moves into high gear.

Next Mr. Stover sends Jason out of the classroom. The consequence, by itself, might have been effective in stopping the disruption, but Mr. Stover doesn't stop there. He adds further humiliation by insisting that Jason write one hundred times "I will not be disrespectful to my teacher." Does this stop the misbehavior? Partially. The disruption is over, but not the power struggle because Jason refuses to write. The scene ends in a standoff.

Yes, punishment did stop Jason's disruptive behavior. Does that prove that punishment is effective? This depends on your definition of effectiveness. If your definition is limited to stopping misbehavior, then punishment usually works. But the cooperation it achieves comes at a very high price: injured feelings, damaged relationships, and angry power struggles.

Punishment is humiliating to children. It hurts their feelings, makes them angry, and incites resistance or fearful withdrawal. Often the hurtful methods are perceived as a personal attack ("You're a bad kid") rather than an attempt to discourage unacceptable behavior ("Your behavior is not acceptable"). The methods obscure the message (Figure 2D).

Imagine how people would respond if our traffic laws were enforced in punitive ways. Visualize yourself driving home. You approach a traffic signal, and the light turns red. There isn't another car in sight, so you take a chance and run the light. As soon as you do, you see a flashing red light in your rearview mirror. The cop pulls you over.

"Are you blind or just stupid?" he asks as he approaches your car. "Couldn't you see the light was red?" He orders you to get out of your car and writes you a citation. But before he hands it to you, he insults you again and hits you twice with his billy club.

Would your response be to say, "Thanks, I needed that. I understand your point, and I'll be sure to stop next time"? Probably not. More likely, you would feel angry and

Figure 2D. The autocratic or punitive approach

Teacher's beliefs	If it doesn't hurt, children won't learn.
	Children won't respect your rules unless they fear your methods.
	It's my job to control my children.
	It's my job to solve my children's problems.
Power and control	All for teachers.
Problem-solving process	Problem solving by force.
	Adversarial.
	Win-lose (teachers win).
	Teachers do all the problem solving and make all the decisions.
	Teachers direct and control the process.
What children learn	Teachers are responsible for solving children's problems.
	Hurtful methods of communication and problem solving.
How children respond	Anger, stubbornness.
	Revenge, rebellion.
	Withdrawal, fearful submission.

resentful. You would understand the rule he was trying to enforce, but you wouldn't feel good about the way the message was communicated. You might even consider ways to get back.

When it comes to being humiliated, kids respond much like adults do. They get angry and resentful. They rebel and seek revenge, and sometimes they withdraw in fearful submission.

If punishment has so many limitations, why then do so many teachers continue to use it? Most teachers who use punishment were raised that way themselves. It feels natural to them, and they don't question its effectiveness. They believe the message has to hurt if the student is going to learn from it. When power struggles develop, they assume the problem is the student, not their methods.

The Mixed Approach (Neither Firm nor Respectful)

As the name implies, the mixed approach is a combination of the punitive and permissive training models. The mixed approach is characterized by inconsistency. Teachers who use it do a lot of flip-flopping back and forth between punishment and permissiveness in search of a better way to get their message across, one that is both firm and respectful. The goal is elusive because they lack the methods to achieve it. So they continue to flip-flop.

There are several variations of the mixed approach. Some teachers start off permissively with lots of repeating, reminding, warnings, and offering second chances, then become frustrated and try punitive tactics—threatening, shaming, blaming, and imposing harsh and drawn-out consequences. Others start off punitively with stern commands, investigation, shaming, blaming, and threats, then give in and take a permissive posture when they encounter resistance.

Still others remain loyal to one approach for longer periods of time. They try permissiveness until they can't stand being ignored or taken advantage of any longer, then they flip-flop and try punishment until they can't stand how tyrannical they sound. Then they flip-flop back to permissiveness. The cycle of flip-flops just takes longer to repeat itself.

How do kids respond to the mixed approach? Let's see what happens when one teacher uses this approach with a group of disruptive seventh graders.

Miss Carey, a first-year teacher, is teaching a geography lesson when a paper airplane whizzes past her shoulder. She turns and sees a group of boys laughing and taking particular pleasure in her annoyance.

"Come on, guys," she says. "There's a lesson going on here. Would you like to join us?" The laughter stops for the moment, and Miss Carey proceeds with her lesson.

Within minutes, Miss Carey hears more laughter and sees Mark sitting at his desk with his jacket zipped up over his head. She waits for him to stop, but he just sits there and pretends to follow along. His buddies can barely control themselves.

"Mark!" exclaims Miss Carey, loud enough to get his attention. He unzips his jacket enough to create a peephole.

"Can I help you?" he asks. His friends continue to laugh.

"You sure can," replies Miss Carey. "You can take your jacket off your head and sit the way you're supposed to. I don't appreciate your clowning around. I really wish you would show a little respect."

"OK," says Mark with a smirk. He sits up rigidly in his seat, chest out, eyes forward, as though he were standing at attention. "Is this better?" he asks.

"You know what I mean," she replies. "I don't want to have to tell you again." Mark relaxes his shoulders slightly, then shoots a quick grin at his buddies. Miss Carey returns to her lesson. Her patience is wearing thin.

A few minutes later, Miss Carey is startled by a loud thud. Mark is lying on the floor next to his desk. Everyone is looking at him.

"I can't believe it!" he exclaims with feigned surprise. "I fell out of my seat! And I was trying so hard to sit the right way, too." He grins at his friends, who can barely control their laughter.

"I've had it!" explodes Miss Carey. "If you insist on acting like a jerk, then do it outside my classroom." She hands him a referral to the office and points to the door. "Take as long as you want, but don't come back until you can figure out how to cooperate. You'll get F grades on everything you miss while you're gone."

Clearly, Mark pushed things to the limit, but did his behavior cause Miss Carey to explode or did she set herself up by allowing things to go too far? Let's answer these questions by examining a diagram of their interaction (Figure 2E).

What happens the first time Mark and buddies disrupt? Do they receive a clear message to stop? No. Miss Carey appeals for their cooperation. She points out that

Figure 2E. Diagram of a mixed interaction

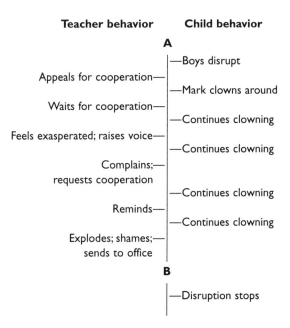

Teacher behavior	Child behavior
	A
	—Boys disrupt
Appeals for cooperation—	
	—Mark clowns around
Waits for cooperation—	
	—Continues clowning
Feels exasperated; raises voice—	
	—Continues clowning
Complains; requests cooperation—	
	—Continues clowning
Reminds—	
	—Continues clowning
Explodes; shames; sends to office—	
	B
	—Disruption stops

45

there is a lesson in progress and invites them to join in. Does this mean they have a choice? If it does, their choice is clear. They continue testing.

What happens the second time Mark disrupts? Does Miss Carey give him a clear signal to stop and tell him what will happen if he doesn't? No. She tells him she doesn't appreciate his behavior and says she wishes he would show a little more respect. What does that mean? How little is too little? Mark gets right to work trying to find out. He continues to disrupt and to be disrespectful.

What happens the third time Mark disrupts? Does he finally get the information he's looking for? No. Miss Carey tells him that she doesn't want to have to tell him again. Tell him what? She probably believes she has been saying stop all along, but she hasn't been saying it in terms that Mark understands. She is trying to be respectful, but her message lacks firmness and clarity.

Let's look at things from Mark's perspective. He really enjoys negative attention. He disrupted class three times, and each time, nothing happened to make him stop. Why should he take Miss Carey seriously? He doesn't. He continues disrupting.

What happens the fourth time? Finally, Miss Carey has had enough. She is ready to act, but she has allowed things to go too far. Her anger and frustration take over. She explodes and ends up using the punitive tactics she tried so hard to avoid. Like many teachers who use the mixed approach, she lacks the methods to be firm and respectful at the same time.

The Democratic Approach (Firm and Respectful)

We've seen that effective guidance requires a balance between firmness and respect. The punitive approach is firm but not respectful. The permissive approach, on the other extreme, is respectful but not firm. The mixed approach is neither firm nor respectful. All three are based on win-lose methods of problem solving and faulty beliefs about learning. None of them teaches responsibility or accomplishes our basic training goals. What, then, is the alternative?

Fortunately, there is an alternative to the extremes of punishment and permissiveness. The democratic approach is a win-win method of problem solving that combines firmness with respect and accomplishes all of our basic training goals. It stops misbehavior. It teaches responsibility. And it conveys, in the clearest way, the lessons we want to teach about our rules for acceptable behavior. Best of all, the democratic approach achieves our goals with less time and energy and without injuring feelings, damaging relationships, or provoking angry power struggles in the process.

The democratic approach succeeds where others fail because the process is cooperative, not adversarial. It focuses on what child guidance is all about—teaching and learning. The teacher's job is to guide the learning process by providing clear limits, acceptable choices, and instructive consequences that hold children accountable for their actions. No threats or detective work. No lecturing or cajoling. No flip-flopping back and forth. And no power struggles. The methods don't hurt. Children are simply provided with the information they need to make acceptable choices about their behavior, then allowed to experience the consequences of those choices.

Does the term *democratic* mean that all guidance decisions are put to a vote and decided by consensus? No. The term is used to describe this approach because children are provided with freedom within well-defined limits and allowed to make decisions about their own behavior. The boundaries are neither too broad nor too restrictive. They permit freedom and choices, but children are given only as much freedom as they can handle responsibly. Let's look at how one teacher uses the democratic approach to handle a problem with class disruption.

Josh and Aaron, two second graders, sit across from each other in the same table group. They're supposed to be working on a handwriting assignment, but they fool around instead. First Josh tosses an eraser at Aaron and hits him in the chest. Aaron flicks it back. Then Josh throws a wad of paper and hits Aaron. When Aaron throws it back, he hits Carly instead. She complains to the teacher.

"Mr. Jordan, Aaron threw something at me."

"Josh threw it at me first," says Aaron.

"No I didn't," says Josh. "You threw an eraser at me."

Mr. Jordan intervenes. "Josh and Aaron, you both should be working quietly on your handwriting assignment. Would you like to work quietly at your desks or by yourselves at the back tables?" He keeps two tables in the back corners of the room for cooldowns, time-outs, or when students need to be separated from their table groups. He looks at each for an answer.

"I want to stay here," says Aaron.

"Me, too," says Josh.

"OK," says Mr. Jordan, "but if there is any more disrupting, you'll have to move to the back tables."

Aaron is convinced. He decides to settle down. Not Josh. He enjoyed the brief soap opera his disruption created, and he's hungry for more. When Mr. Jordan walks away, Josh fires off several more paper wads at Aaron. One hits Aaron in the head. The other sails over Aaron's shoulder and catches Mr. Jordan's attention.

"Pick up your assignment, Josh," says Mr. Jordan matter-of-factly. "You'll have to finish at the back table." Josh heads off to complete the lesson by himself. The disruption is over.

Unlike the teachers in my previous examples, Mr. Jordan succeeds in a firm and respectful manner. He achieves all of his guidance goals and maintains positive relationships in the process. No lectures. No humiliating consequences. No flip-flopping and no angry power struggles. He simply gives the boys the information they need to cooperate, then follows through based on their choice. Let's take a closer look at his methods by examining a diagram of the interaction (Figure 2F).

Notice how short this diagram is. Effective guidance requires less time and energy and achieves better results. Mr. Jordan is working with a plan. He knows what he's going to do, and he's prepared for whatever resistance he may encounter.

He begins at point A by giving the boys a clear message about what he expects. He tells them they should be working quietly on their writing assignment. Then he gives them some choices. He asks if they would like to work quietly at their seats or at the back tables. Both boys say they want to work at their seats. So Mr. Jordan tells them they will have to move if there is any further disrupting.

Now the boys have all the information they need to make an acceptable decision. They know what's expected and what will happen if they choose not to cooperate. The

Figure 2F. Diagram of a democratic interaction

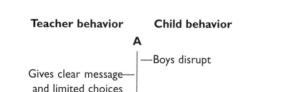

way things are set up, they cannot avoid learning the lesson Mr. Jordan intends.

What happens? Aaron decides to cooperate, but not Josh. He decides to test and continues disrupting. So Mr. Jordan simply follows through. In a matter-of-fact manner, he requests Josh to take his work to the back table and fin-

Figure 2G. The democratic approach

Teacher's beliefs	Children are capable of solving problems on their own.
	Children should be given choices and allowed to learn from the consequences of their choices.
	Encouragement is an effective way to motivate cooperation.
Power and control	Children are given only as much power and control as they can handle responsibly.
Problem-solving process	Cooperative.
	Win-win.
	Based on mutual respect.
	Children are active participants in the problem-solving process.
What children learn	Responsibility.
	Cooperation.
	Independence.
	Respect for rules and authority.
	Self-control.
How children respond	More cooperation.
	Less limit testing.
	Resolve problems on their own.
	Regard teacher's words seriously.

ish up. Josh gets a very clear message. Mr. Jordan is teaching his rules effectively.

Can you imagine how much more rewarding your teaching would be without all the reminders, threats, lectures, and power struggles? The goal is achievable. The methods are simple and easy to learn. The hardest part is recognizing the things that aren't working for you (Figure 2G).

In the chapters that follow, you'll discover the type of limits you're using and why children respond to you the way they do. With an awareness of what hasn't worked for you, you'll be ready to say good-bye to old ineffective methods and learn new skills.

Chapter

3

How Children Learn Your Rules

Each day when it's time to line up for recess, Anthony pushes and shoves his way to the front of the line. Then when the bell rings, he sprints down the hallway, sometimes crashing into others, in an attempt to be first to arrive at the tetherball poles.

"I've told him over and over again that it's not OK to push in line or run down the hallway," complains his frustrated teacher, "but he does it day after day. I've explained how dangerous his behavior is. I've even asked his parents to talk to him. Nothing seems to help. I'm beginning to think he has some type of learning problem."

Anthony's teacher believes she is teaching a rule, but Anthony is not learning the rule she is trying to teach. This chapter will show you why. You'll discover how children learn your rules and why the teaching and learning process sometimes breaks down. By the time you're done, you'll be a step closer to teaching your rules in the clearest and most understandable way. Let's look at how Christi's teacher does it.

Christi, age four, pretends to cook breakfast in the miniature kitchen in her preschool room. Her friend Beth sits at a small table waiting to be served.

"Would you like some eggs?" asks Christi.

"Yes, please," replies Beth. Christi pretends to scoop the eggs onto a plastic plate, but the pan slips from her hand and falls in Beth's lap. Both girls laugh. Things start to get silly.

"You spilled eggs all over me!" says Beth, still laughing. She grabs her cup and pretends to pour juice over Christi's head. Both laugh. Things get even sillier. Christi picks up a plastic toaster and swings it over her head by the cord. She nearly hits Beth in the head.

"Put the toaster down, Christi," says her teacher matter-of-factly. "You can play with it the right way, or I'll have to put it away."

Christi hears the words, but she's very excited. She continues to swing the toaster. Her teacher reaches over and takes the toaster away. "You can play with it later this afternoon," she says, "if you play with it the right way."

Christi is learning her teacher's rules about using the play items in the classroom. She may need to repeat this lesson before she masters the rule, but her teacher's methods will certainly lead to the desired outcome.

Christi's teacher is teaching her rules effectively. Her words say stop, and her actions convey the same message when she takes the toaster away. When our words are consistent with our actions, we don't need a lot of words or harsh consequences to get our message across. Our message is clear, and so is the rule behind it.

Children Learn Concretely

Jean Piaget's research on children's intellectual development has shown that the thinking and learning of children is qualitatively different from that of adults. Children think and learn concretely. For younger children, immediate sensory experience plays a greater role in shaping their reality than for adolescents or adults.

What does this mean to teachers in the classroom? It means that children's beliefs are largely determined by what they experience with their senses. What they see, hear, touch, and feel determines how they think things are. Their perceptions and beliefs about how the world works are based primarily on their concrete experiences.

Piaget's findings have important implications for how we go about teaching our rules to children. We do this in two basic ways—with our words and with our actions. Both teach a lesson, but only our actions are concrete. Actions, not words, define our rules.

For example, if I tell my ten-year-old son that it's not OK to kick the soccer ball in the house, but he does it anyway, and I overlook it, what is he learning about my rule? Of course, he's learning that it's really OK to kick the ball in the house.

If, on the other hand, I take the ball away each time he kicks it in the house, he and I would probably share the same belief about my rule. He would know that I meant what I said.

When our words match our actions consistently, children learn to take our words seriously and to recognize the rules behind them. When our words do not match our actions, however, children learn to ignore our words and to base their beliefs on what they experience. In effect, we are teaching two rules: a rule in theory and a rule in practice.

This essential miscommunication is the source of most breakdowns in the teaching and learning process, and most adults are not even aware that it's happening. They continue to teach their rules with words while their children learn by actions. This is what was happening to Anthony and his teacher in our opening example, and this is what is taking place in many classrooms throughout the country.

Why Limits Are Important

Limits are the messages or signals we use to communicate our rules and expectations for behavior. Limits answer some very basic questions children ask about how their world works. On the surface, limits operate like traffic signals by providing information in the form of green lights (do that) and red lights (stop that) for acceptable and unacceptable behavior. These signals answer the questions: "What's OK?" and "What's not OK?"

Beneath the surface, however, limits answer a very different set of questions about the power and authority of the person sending the messages: "Who's in control?" "How far can I go?" "What happens when I go too far?" The answers to these questions define the balance of power and authority in teacher-student relationships and help children determine whether compliance with their teacher's rules is optional or really required.

Limit-Testing: Children's Research

How do children clarify our rules and expectations? How do they determine if what we ask is really expected and required? Rarely do they come up and ask, "How much power and authority do you really have? How do I know you really mean what you say? And what are you going to do if I don't do what you ask?" My guess is that you probably haven't had this experience very often, if at all.

Most children don't ask these questions with their words, but they do think about them, and they do ask them with their behavior. They just go ahead and do whatever we asked them not to do, then they wait to see what happens. This is limit-testing behavior, and this is how children do their research. It answers their basic questions more definitively than words. Much of what we consider to be misbehavior in the classroom is actually limit testing or children's attempts to clarify what we really expect.

Temperament affects the way children conduct their research. For example, compliant children are eager to please. They do not require a lot of hard data or action messages to be convinced to follow our rules. When they hear us say, "Stop," they think compliant thoughts such as "I really should." Most are willing to accept our words as all the data they need and cooperate for the asking. Compliant children don't do a lot of testing.

Strong-willed children, on the other hand, conduct their research more aggressively. They require a lot of hard data to be convinced that we really mean what we say. When they hear us say "Stop," they're thinking: "Or what? What will happen if I don't?" They know how to find out. They test. Strong-willed children need to experience what we say repeatedly before they are convinced we really mean it.

Strong-willed children are more determined to train us than we are to train them. As a result, we have to work hard to get our message across. Whatever methods we use to do that, we will need to use them more often. If we use punishment, we will have to punish harder and more frequently. If we use permissiveness, we will have to do a lot more reminding and persuading. The quickest way to discover what's not working for you is to match your guidance methods with a strong-willed child.

You've probably noticed examples of how temperament and research styles differ among your students or perhaps even among members of your own family. I have. My oldest son, Scott, is usually compliant. He cooperates for the asking. My youngest son, Ian, is strong willed. He requires hard data before he is convinced I mean business. My boys do their research differently, and I've learned to adjust my signals accordingly.

For example, both boys like to listen to the TV with the volume cranked up. When Scott does this, I simply say, "Scott, the TV is too loud. Turn it down please." He always does, at least he has so far, and I've learned to count on his cooperation. He accepts my words as all the data he needs.

If I use the same message with Ian, I know from experience what he's likely to do. He will just sit there and ignore me and wait for a clearer signal. Or, he might give me the words I want to hear and say, "I will," but continue to do what he wants. This isn't really lying. What Ian really means is "I will when I have to, and I didn't hear that I have to."

Like many strong-willed kids, Ian is thinking, "Or what?" He's looking for concrete, definitive information about what I really expect. So I've learned to provide him with all the data he needs to make an acceptable choice. When the TV is on too loud, I say, "Ian, turn the TV down, please, or I'll have to turn it off."

Now Ian has all the data he needs to make an acceptable choice. He knows what I expect, and he knows what will happen if he doesn't cooperate. His research questions are answered. He usually turns it down.

Aggressive Researchers

My job as a child therapist brings me into frequent contact with the most aggressive researchers in a large school district. I see the kids who don't stop at the signals their teachers hold up in the classroom, the ones who push everything to the limit. Loren, a second grader, is a good example. He was referred after a series of suspensions for disruptive and uncooperative behavior in the classroom.

"Loren won't listen to anyone," commented his teacher. "He thinks he can do whatever he wants. I've had numerous conferences with his parents, and they say he acts the same way at home. We're all at a loss for what to do."

When Loren arrived at my office with his parents, he plopped himself down in one of my comfortable blue swivel chairs and began sizing me up. Then he went right to work on me. We hadn't exchanged a word, but his research was under way.

What do you think Loren and many other children do when they first sit in my chairs? Right. They spin them, and sometimes they put their feet in them, too. They know it's not OK. Their parents know it, and so do I, but the kids do it anyway. They look at me, then at their parents, and go ahead and see what happens. This is limit-testing behavior. When it happens, I know I am about to learn a great deal about how the family communicates about limits.

I don't need behavior rating scales, standardized tests, or lengthy clinical interviews to see what's going on. I just watch the child, the chairs, and the parents for ten to fifteen minutes, and I usually have all the information I need to see what's going on.

Loren's parents responded to his chair spinning the way most permissive parents do. They ignored it. They pretended it wasn't happening and focused instead on telling me about all of the disruptive things Loren did at school. Loren continued spinning. Five minutes passed. Not one signal had been given.

Ten minutes into our session, I could see Loren's father was becoming annoyed. He made his first attempt at a signal. He said Loren's name softly and gave him a look of disapproval.

Loren did what most kids do when this happens. He acknowledged the gesture, stopped briefly, then resumed his spinning as soon as his father looked away. Loren and his parents were reenacting a script, the same one they go through dozens of times each week whenever Loren misbehaves.

With his behavior, Loren was asking the same questions he asks at home and in the classroom: "What's OK? What's not OK? Who's in control? How far can I go? And what happens when I go too far?" He knew his parents weren't going to do anything about his behavior, so he was conducting his research to determine my power and authority and the rules that operated in my office. Between disapproving looks from his father, Loren continued to spin. I waited to see what would happen next.

A few more minutes passed, then Loren's father did what many other parents do at this point. He reached over and stopped the chair with his hand. His signal elicited the same response as before. Loren acknowledged the gesture, waited for his father to remove his hand, then continued spinning.

Loren's parents were doing their best to say stop, but Loren knew from experience that stopping was not really expected or required. All of the gestures were just steps in a well-rehearsed drama. The spinning continued. I could see why he wasn't responding to his teacher's signals in the classroom.

Fifteen minutes went by, and Loren still had not received a clear signal from his parents. Their anger was apparent. Finally his exasperated mother turned to me and said, "See what he does! This is the same thing we have to put up with at home!"

At this point, I intervened and helped Loren answer some of his research questions. In a matter-of-fact voice, I said, "Loren, I'd like you to use my blue chairs, but I have two rules you'll have to follow—don't spin them and don't put your feet in them. I'm confident you can follow my rules, but if you don't, you'll have to sit in my orange chair for the rest of the session." I keep an old plastic orange chair in my office for these situations.

What do you think Loren did? Sure, he did the same thing most strong-willed children do. He tested. Not right away, but within a few minutes, he gave the chair another spin and looked for my reaction. He heard my words, now he wanted hard data. He wanted to see what I would do.

So I did what I always do when this happens. I pulled out the orange chair and said calmly, "This will be your chair for the rest of the session. You can try my blue chairs again next session." Then I stood next to him and waited for him to move with a look of expectation. Reluctantly, Loren moved into the orange chair.

What did Loren and I just work out? I just answered his research questions. He heard stop, and he experienced stopping. Now he knows what I expect and what will happen if he decides to test the next time he visits my office. Loren has all the information he needs to make an acceptable choice.

You're probably wondering what happens when children refuse to get out of the blue chair. The interesting thing is that most don't test when they get the information they need to make an acceptable choice. I see more than a hundred chair spinners a year in my counseling work. Only a few continue to test when I bring out the orange chair.

What happens when they do? The process is still the same. The questions haven't changed. They are still asking: "Or what? What are you going to do about it?" So I try to give them the data they're looking for in the same matter-of-fact manner. I turn to their parents and say, "Your child doesn't want to get out of my chair. Do I have your permission to move him?"

In ten years, I've never had a parent say no. Most are so embarrassed over their child's behavior, they can't wait to get out of my office. Others are very curious to see if I can actually get their child to cooperate.

Once I get their permission, I turn to the child and say, "Your parents say I can move you into the orange chair, but I'd prefer that you move yourself. What would you like to do?" I take a few deep breaths and wait patiently for fifteen or twenty seconds.

What do you think they do? A very few, maybe two or three each year, wait until I get up out of my chair before they are convinced I will act. Then they move into the other chair. The vast majority move on their own. Why? They move because they have all the information they need to make an acceptable decision. Their questions are answered. Even aggressive researchers can make acceptable choices when provided with clear signals. Their cooperation demonstrates the power of a clear message.

When children like Loren misbehave at school, the focus is on their problem behavior not the hidden forces that operate beneath the surface to shape that problem behavior. This is where my investigative work begins. I try to determine why the teaching and learning process breaks down. Is the problem teaching? Or learning? Or is something else going on? I try to answer these questions by examining the ways rules are taught both at home and in the classroom.

Permissive Rules

Permissive guidance methods often lead to breakdowns in the teaching and learning process because teachers confuse their words for actions and become frustrated when their message doesn't get across. Children learn a different rule than their teacher intends.

For example, Barry, a third grader, tilts back precariously in his chair while his teacher gives a lesson at the board. She notices and gives him a disapproving look. He straightens his chair briefly, but as soon as she looks away, he tilts back once again.

"He's not really hurting anything," his teacher says to herself. She decides to ignore it, and Barry continues to tilt. Ten minutes pass. Then he slips and nearly falls before catching himself.

"That doesn't look very safe to me," says his teacher. "I'm afraid you might hurt yourself. I'd feel more comfortable if you sat the right way."

"I'll be careful," says Barry.

"I know you will," she replies, "but accidents can happen even when you're careful, and I'd hate to see you get hurt. Please sit the right way, OK?" She waits for Barry to comply. He does, and she returns to her lesson, satisfied that her message got across.

It doesn't take long before Barry tests again. This time, he props his feet on the rails of his desk to stabilize his chair while tilting. When his teacher sees what's going on, she feels frustrated.

"I thought I asked you to sit the right way," she says with irritation. "What would the principal say if she walked into our classroom and saw you sitting like that?"

"But it's safe the way I'm doing it," argues Barry. He demonstrates how he can stabilize his chair by putting his feet on the sides of his desk.

"I'm still not comfortable with it," says the teacher. "I'm going to have to insist that you stop."

"OK," says Barry reluctantly, "but I don't see what it's hurting." He stops tilting.

Do you think Barry and his teacher are done with this issue? Barry's teacher sincerely believes she's saying stop when she points out the dangers of tilting back in the chair. She becomes frustrated and annoyed when he does not respond as expected. In actuality, she is communicating two messages, but she is aware of only one.

Her words say something that resembles stop, but what does Barry experience? He doesn't experience stopping. Instead, he hears more talking. His teacher's action message is really saying: "Go ahead and do what you want. I don't like it, but I'm not going to do anything about it, at least not for a while."

Barry responds to the mixed message like many children do. He ignores the words and continues pushing with his behavior. He learns from what he experiences. What is Barry's interpretation of his teacher's rule? Sure, it's OK to tilt back in his chair as long as he can tolerate his teacher's attempts to persuade him not to.

Punitive Rules

Those who operate from the punitive model use both words and actions to teach their rules, but their methods often end up teaching a different lesson than they intend. This is what Mr. Silva experienced when he tried to handle a problem with one of his sixth graders.

Mr. Silva is writing instructions for an upcoming literature assignment when he hears a clicking sound coming from the middle of the room. He turns and sees several students looking at Mel who slouches in his seat.

"Mel, what you're doing is not respectful," says Mr. Silva.

"It wasn't me," Mel replies.

"Don't lie to me!" says Mr. Silva. "Now sit up and pay attention. If I hear any more noises out of you, you'll spend your next recess on the bench."

"What a jerk," Mel murmurs under his breath.

"What was that, Mel?" inquires Mr. Silva angrily. "Would you like to say it a little louder for others to hear?"

"I didn't say anything," Mel replies.

"Oh yes you did," accuses Mr. Silva. "Whatever it was, I'm sure it was disrespectful. You just earned a recess on the bench. Your smart mouth got you in trouble again."

"Oh ouch! That really hurts," says Mel sarcastically.

"You've just earned another recess on the bench," says Mr. Silva angrily. "Wanna try for three?" Mel clutches his chest in mock agony. "That's three!" says Mr. Silva. "How about all the recesses for the week?"

Mel is tempted to retaliate, but he believes Mr. Silva will follow through on his threat. Mel does not want to lose his recesses. He sits and glares his defiance.

Mr. Silva doesn't realize it, but he is teaching two rules about being disrespectful in the classroom. His words (rule in theory) say "It's not OK," but what kind of behavior is he modeling? His actions (rule in practice) say just the opposite. He is teaching the same behavior he's trying to eliminate. Which lesson is Mel following?

Lessons at Home
Affect Lessons at School

The home is the training ground for the real world. That's where children first learn the rules for acceptable behavior. They take those lessons with them into the classroom. Steven is a good example. When I first met him, he had been suspended from school four times for hitting, and it was October. The year had barely begun.

His fourth-grade teacher tried everything she knew to help Steven change. She explained the school's rules about hitting. She encouraged him to ask an adult for help whenever he got into a conflict, and she offered her assistance when Steven got into conflicts in the classroom. Nothing helped. She was frustrated, and so were Steven's parents.

"Living with Steven is like being around a time bomb waiting to explode," said his mother. "He knows that hitting is not OK, but he does it anyway. He hits his younger brother, he hits other kids in the neighborhood, and he hits kids at school. We've talked to him over and over again, but it doesn't seem to sink in."

"What exactly do you say to him when he hits others?" I asked, curious about their verbal messages.

"Well, I get a little loud," confessed Steven's father. "It makes me angry to see Steven mistreating others, and I let him know I'm not going to tolerate it."

"What do you do to get that message across?" I asked.

"We paddle him when he needs it," Steven's father replied. "We don't believe in all this permissive stuff going on today. Kids need to know you mean business."

"How many times a week does Steven need that kind of reminder?" I asked.

"Two or three times, and sometimes more. He needs to know when he's gone too far," said his father.

"With that many reminders, why do you think Steven is having such a difficult time learning your rules?" I asked.

"We suspect he has some kind of a learning problem," Steven's mother replied. "We're considering having him tested."

As I got to know Steven, I could see he didn't need testing. The problem wasn't learning. It was teaching. Steven was a very capable learner. He was mastering all the lessons his parents were teaching about hurtful problem solving. He was good at yelling, threatening, and intimidating. He knew how to hit, and he was becoming skillful at blaming others when he got caught.

Steven understood his parent's words, but their spoken rules were not the ones they practiced. What did they practice? Hitting. Steven was learning a lesson in violent problem solving. At school he was simply following the lessons he had been taught.

Permissive training at home also sets kids up for problems at school. James is a good example. He was getting off to a rough start in kindergarten when I first met him. The note his teacher sent was revealing: "James pushes everything to the limit. When I ask him to join an activity, he ignores me and does what he wants. When I insist, he cries or throws a tantrum. He seems to think the classroom rules don't apply to him."

James's mother was equally frustrated. "He's the same way at home," she complained. "He refuses to get dressed in the morning. He won't come in when I call him, and getting him to bed is a nightmare by itself. I have to ask him over and over again. Most of the time, he just ignores me and does what he wants."

Like many children trained with permissiveness, James was accustomed to getting his own way, and he had developed a full repertoire of skills to make that happen. He was an expert at tuning out, ignoring, resisting, avoiding, arguing, debating, bargaining, challenging, and defying. If those tactics didn't work, James played his trump card. He threw a tantrum. His mother usually felt guilty and gave in.

James's intentions were not malicious. He did it because it worked. His experiences had taught him that "Rules are for others, not me. I make my own rules, and I do what I want." James operated on these beliefs both at home and in the classroom.

It wasn't hard to understand why James had such an exaggerated perception of his own power and authority and why he was doing so much testing. At home the stop signals he confronted did not require stopping, and no really meant yes most of the time. When he misbehaved, he knew he would hear a lot of repeating, reminding, lecturing, and threatening, but none of those methods required stopping. His training had not prepared him for the real stop signs he was encountering in the classroom.

Teaching Rules Effectively

Teachers can't control the faulty lessons children learn at home, but they can help children move in a more acceptable direction by teaching their rules effectively in the classroom. Let's look at how one teacher does it.

Katy, a third grader, loves to play four square, but she doesn't like to follow the rules. Sometimes when her turn is over, she refuses to leave the court.

"She's cheating again," several kids complain when Mrs. Karim arrives on the scene. "She won't leave when her turn is over." Katy stands in the court with her hands on her hips refusing to budge.

"You're going to have to play by the rules, Katy, or find a different game to play," says Mrs. Karim matter-of-factly. "What would you like to do?"

"OK," says Katy as she heads to the end of the line. The game resumes, but within minutes the kids complain again. Mrs. Karim sees Katy standing in the court refusing to leave.

"I won't do it again," says Katy when she sees Mrs. Karim.

"That's a good choice," replies Mrs. Karim, "but you're going to have to find a different game to play this morning. You can try four square again this afternoon." No shaming. No blaming. No harsh words or lectures. Katy hears the same message she experiences. She may need several more of these experiences before she masters the intended rule, but the methods will surely lead to the desired outcome.

Mr. Givens also is effective when he sees one of his ninth-grade students reading a magazine in class.

"Seth, magazines don't belong in class," says Mr. Givens matter-of-factly.

"I'm not disturbing anybody," says Seth, looking for a little bargaining room. Mr. Givens doesn't take the bait.

"You can put it away in your backpack," Mr. Givens replies, "or I will keep it in my desk until the end of the semester."

Now Seth has all the information he needs to make an acceptable decision. He knows what's expected and what will happen if he decides to test. The way things are set up, Mr. Givens cannot fail to get his message across. There are no payoffs for aggressive research.

Chapter Summary

Children learn concretely. Their beliefs and perceptions are based primarily on what they experience, not necessarily on what they are told. This fact has important implications for how we go about teaching our rules. We do it in two basic ways—with our words and with our actions. Both teach a lesson, but only our actions are concrete. Actions, not words, define our rules.

When our words match our actions consistently, children learn to trust our words and recognize the rules behind them. When our words do not match our actions, however, children learn to ignore our words and base their beliefs on what they experience. In reality, they are learning two sets of rules—our spoken rules and the rules we practice.

This fundamental miscommunication about rules is why many well-intended guidance lessons break down. Most teachers are unaware it's even happening. They just continue to try to get their message across with their words while their students learn from what they experience.

Children are skillful at determining whether our spoken rules are also the rules we practice. They test. Limit testing is how children conduct their research. Compliant children do not need a lot of data to be convinced to follow our rules. Strong-willed children, on the other hand, are much more aggressive researchers. They need a lot of data to be convinced that our spoken rules are actually the ones we practice.

We can help children complete their research and learn our rules by providing the signals they understand best—clear words and effective actions. These tools are the key to teaching our rules in the clearest and most understandable way.

▼
Chapter
4

The Classroom Dance

Teachers who operate with unclear or ineffective limits develop their own special dance of miscommunication, which they perform over and over again when their rules are tested or violated. There's a permissive version of the dance that's wordy and drawn out and a punitive version that's angrier and more dramatic. Some teachers do a little of both. All dances are exercises in ineffective communication that lead to escalating conflicts and power struggles. Over time, the dances become such a familiar and deeply ingrained habit that teachers experience them as their normal way of doing things. They are not even aware they are dancing.

Teachers such as the ones we'll follow in this chapter can easily become stuck in these destructive patterns of communication. Without awareness and new skills, there's no way out. They have no choice but to continue dancing the only dance they know. Awareness is the key to breaking free.

If you suspect that you've been dancing with your students, this chapter will help you break free. You'll learn how your dances begin, how they end, and what keeps them going. Most important, you'll learn how to step off the dance floor so you can move on to more effective forms of communication. Let's look at how one frustrated teacher discovered her dance.

A Permissive Dance

Barbara, a third-grade teacher, was on the verge of burnout when I first met her. Her third year of teaching was starting off as rough as the previous two. The thought of facing another year full of conflicts and power struggles was more than she could bear. Depression was sinking in. Her principal suggested that she give me a call.

"I became a teacher because I like kids," Barbara said when she arrived at my office, "but I don't enjoy them much anymore. I treat them with kindness and respect, but some of them just tune me out and do what they want. I nag them all day long. They're wearing me out!"

She didn't realize it, but Barbara was stuck in an escalating pattern of conflicts and power struggles that she believed the kids were causing. My first task was to help her recognize her dance.

"Pick a typical misbehavior in your classroom and describe, in a very step-by-step manner, exactly what you say and do when your students behave this way."

"The most persistent problem I face is all the talking and clowning around that goes on while I'm teaching. This drives me up a wall."

"What do you when this happens?" I asked. As she described what usually happens, I diagrammed each step in the interactional sequence. Visual diagrams are an effective way to help teachers get acquainted with their dance. When Barbara finished, we both took a moment to reflect on her diagram (Figure 4A).

"Look familiar?" I asked.

"I must go through that ten times a day," said Barbara. "See what I mean when I say I nag them all day long." She looked exhausted.

"Yes, that's quite a dance," I replied, giving it the label it deserved. I could understand why she felt so worn-out.

Classroom dances are like saving stress coupons. If we collect enough of them in the course of a day or a week, we get a prize—headaches, stomachaches, and a variety of other upsets, even depression and burnout. Barbara's coupon book was full.

Figure 4A. Barbara's diagram

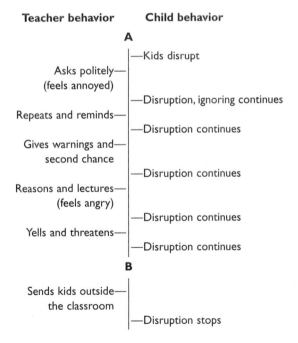

Teacher behavior	Child behavior
	A
	—Kids disrupt
Asks politely— (feels annoyed)	
	—Disruption, ignoring continues
Repeats and reminds—	
	—Disruption continues
Gives warnings and— second chance	
	—Disruption continues
Reasons and lectures— (feels angry)	
	—Disruption continues
Yells and threatens—	
	—Disruption continues
	B
Sends kids outside— the classroom	
	—Disruption stops

"Let's make sure we've captured everything that happens in your diagram," I said. "At what point in the dance do you begin to feel annoyed?"

"I'm annoyed from the beginning," she replied. "I know they're not going to cooperate, but I don't show my anger until later on. I try reasoning and lecturing, then I wear down, and my anger comes out. That's when I get loud."

At the beginning of Barbara's diagram, I wrote the words "feels annoyed," then, after her lecturing step, I wrote the words "feels angry." The sequence of events was now complete.

So I summarized what Barbara's diagram was telling us. "It seems that the more you talk, the more the kids tune you out, and the angrier you become. Your dance continues until you can't take any more. Then you stop it with your action step." Barbara nodded in agreement.

Her diagram was revealing. She started off with a polite request to stop. Her requests were usually ignored. Then she tried repeating and reminding followed by warnings and second chances. The misbehavior continued. So she shifted gears again and tried reasoning and lecturing. The resistance continued.

The more she talked, the angrier she became until reasoning and lecturing turned into yelling and threats. When she reached her breaking point, she made disruptive students stand outside the classroom, ending the dance. Repeat offenders were sent to the office.

I returned to Barbara's diagram and drew a circle around all the steps that used words. This took up nearly all of her diagram. I labeled these "verbal steps." Then I drew a box around the step that involved action and labeled this "action step." The box occupied only a small portion of her diagram (Figure 4B).

"Which steps take up most of your time and energy and cause you the greatest frustration?" I asked. She pointed to her verbal steps.

Figure 4B. Barbara's verbal and action steps

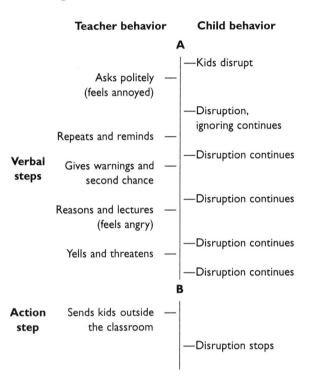

	Teacher behavior	Child behavior
		A
		—Kids disrupt
	Asks politely — (feels annoyed)	
		—Disruption, ignoring continues
	Repeats and reminds —	
		—Disruption continues
Verbal steps	Gives warnings and — second chance	
		—Disruption continues
	Reasons and lectures — (feels angry)	
		—Disruption continues
	Yells and threatens —	
		—Disruption continues
		B
Action step	Sends kids outside — the classroom	
		—Disruption stops

"Now, which steps stopped the misbehavior?" I asked. She just looked at me and smiled. She didn't need to answer because the answer stood right in front of her. Her diagram was proof that she spent most of her time and energy doing things that didn't work. Barbara looked confused and relieved at the same time.

"I thought I was supposed to do all that stuff," she confessed as she pointed to the circled portion of her diagram. "I thought I was giving them every opportunity to cooperate, but I can see I was giving them opportunities not to cooperate."

The insight would be her ticket out of the dances. The hardest part was now behind her. She recognized what wasn't working for her. My next task was to help her understand the type of research she was encountering.

"Imagine that you're eight years old," I suggested. "You're skillful at wearing people down and getting your way. When you hear someone say stop, your first thought is 'Or what? What will happen if I don't?' Now let's look at your diagram. At what point do you answer these questions?"

"When I send them outside the room," she replied.

"Right," I said. "Your action step answers their research questions. There is no further need for testing." Barbara could see that the kids pushed because she was willing to bend. When she held firm, the pushing stopped. Her ineffective attempts to say stop were beginning to sink in.

"The kids probably get other payoffs from your dances," I suggested. "If you were only eight years old and you could get an adult to do all this stuff by just tuning out and resisting, would you feel powerful? Do you think you might enjoy the entertainment and negative attention?"

"OK, I'm convinced," said Barbara. "How do I get out of these dances?"

"You've already taken the most important step by recognizing your dance," I said. "Next, you'll need to eliminate all of your ineffective verbal steps. Your dances will end when you put your words and actions closer together." I returned to her original diagram and posed a question.

"What would happen if you gave your aggressive researchers all the information they needed at point A, then moved on directly to your action step at point B if they tested? No repeating. No reminding. No warnings or second chances. No reasoning or lecturing. No raised voices or threats. None of the steps that waste valuable instructional time and wear you out. Your new message might sound like this: 'Guys, you can follow along quietly or

Figure 4C. Barbara's new diagram

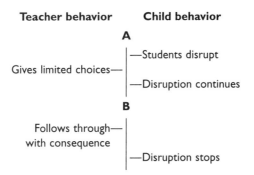

you'll have to spend some quiet time by yourselves. What would you like to do?' "

"I'm ready to give it a try," Barbara replied. Her new diagram soon looked like Figure 4C. So can yours.

A Punitive Dance

Punitive dances tend to be louder, angrier, and more dramatic than their permissive counterparts. The steps are different, but the dances are just another variation of the basic classroom power struggle. They begin with unclear or ineffective messages about rules. They're fueled by anger and resistance, and they lead to escalating conflicts and power struggles.

I recall one punitive dance I witnessed firsthand when a sixth-grade teacher invited me to her classroom to observe one of her disruptive students. "Try to arrive about forty-five minutes before we break for lunch," Sharon suggested on the phone. "Richard usually blows about that time."

She was right. Within minutes of my arrival, Richard disrupted the class. I watched him position several textbooks near the edge of his desk. Then, while Sharon was explaining a math problem at the board, he gave the books a nudge with his elbow. The ensuing crash got everybody's attention.

Sharon turned and glared at him. Her jaw was set. Her hands were on her hips. "That was real smart, Richard!" she said with a disgusted look on her face. "Why don't you grow up and cooperate for a change." She wrote his name on the blackboard under the frown face.

"Give me a break. It was an accident," said Richard with a sly smile.

"Sure it was," said Sharon sarcastically. "Just like all your accidents. I know what you're doing." She glared at him again.

"What?" Richard countered, trying to keep the verbal sparring match going.

"Don't play innocent with me," said Sharon. "I'm sick of your lousy attitude."

"My lousy attitude!" exclaimed Richard, rolling his eyes. "What about yours?"

"That's enough!" said Sharon sharply. "I won't tolerate any more disrespect." She went to the blackboard and wrote a check after his name. "That's your final warning."

"Oh yeah!" Richard sneered. "What are you going to do? Take my recesses away?" It was only Tuesday, but Richard had already lost all of his recess privileges for the week.

"No. You'll go to the office," replied Sharon. "Keep it up if that's what you want."

"It's better than being here!" Richard shot back.

"I'm glad you like it," countered Sharon, "because that's where you're going." She handed him three sheets of paper. "Don't come back until these pages are full of sentences saying 'I will not be disrespectful to my teacher.'" Richard gave her a defiant look as he headed out the door.

When the bell rang for recess, Sharon and I had an opportunity to talk. "See what I have to put up with," she began. "He makes me so angry! I never would have talked to my teachers the way he talks to me."

"Was his behavior today typical of what happens?" I asked.

"Yes," she replied, "but he usually stops when I threaten to send him to the office. He hates that almost as much as being sent home. Nothing else seems to matter to him. I've taken away all of his recesses and free activity time, even his field trips."

"Have you spoken with Richard's parents?" I inquired.

"Yes. We're using a daily behavior report card system," she replied. "Each day, I send a behavior report card home to his parents. If he gets sent to the office, his parents make him spend all of his after-school time in his room. No TV, no video games, and no play privileges."

"Has that helped?" I asked.

"We thought it would," said Sharon, "but his behavior is worse, not better." They were digging themselves in deeper with their drawn-out consequences.

I was curious about how Sharon perceived her guidance methods. "What do you usually do when Richard misbehaves?" I asked.

"The first time, I write his name on the board to call his attention to his behavior and give him a chance to correct it. The second time, I write a check after his name as an additional warning. The third time, he loses a recess. The fourth time, he loses all of his recesses for the day. If he misbehaves again that day, and he usually does, then he loses all of his recesses for the week. Next, I send him to the office to write sentences or an apology letter. If Richard is sent to the office twice on the same day, the principal suspends him for the rest of the day. He has been suspended three times this year."

The methods Sharon described were only a partial description of what I observed. "Is she aware of what she's doing?" I wondered. It was time to hold up a mirror and help her to see the methods she actually used.

"Sometimes visual diagrams give us a clearer picture of what's going on," I suggested. "Earlier, when Richard misbehaved, I recorded what he said and did. Then I recorded your responses. May I draw a descriptive diagram of the interaction?" She nodded.

I went to the blackboard and drew a diagram of the interaction I observed, explaining each step as I went. When I finished, I stood back and gave Sharon a chance to check it over (Figure 4D).

Figure 4D. Sharon's diagram

"Did I do all of that?" she asked in disbelief, as she pointed to the long series of verbal steps in her diagram. "It seems so angry."

"I call them classroom dances," I said. "The dance you do with Richard is an angry one. You both took quite a few shots at each other." My suspicions were confirmed. She wasn't aware of all the steps she used.

"Let's make sure we've captured everything that happens in your dance," I said. "At what point do you become angry?"

"I'm angry in the beginning," Sharon admitted. "I know what usually follows, but I become angriest when he argues and talks back." I returned to her diagram and wrote the words "feels angry" at the beginning of the interaction and the words "feels very angry" during the arguing and verbal sparring.

Sharon's diagram was now complete, so I summarized what it was telling us. "Richard is skillful at hooking you into verbal sparring matches. The more you talk, the more resistance you encounter, and the angrier you become. Your dance continues to heat up until you finally stop it with your action step."

"Let's take a look at the various steps in your dance," I suggested. I returned to Sharon's diagram and drew a circle around all the steps that relied primarily on words. I labeled these "verbal steps." They took up most of her diagram. Next, I drew a box around all the steps that involved action and labeled these "action steps." They took up a small section at the end of her diagram (Figure 4E).

"You use two types of steps to stop Richard's misbehavior: verbal steps and action steps." I said. "Which one always stops his misbehavior?"

"My action steps," Sharon replied.

"Right," I said. "Sometimes he stops when you threaten to send him to the office because he knows from experience that your action steps will follow."

4E. Sharon's verbal and action steps

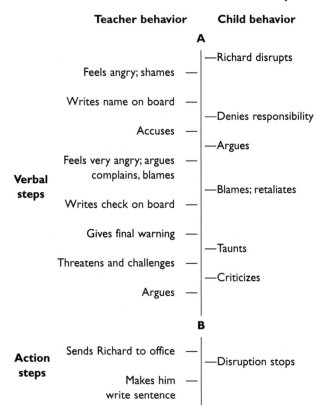

	Teacher behavior		Child behavior
		A	
			—Richard disrupts
	Feels angry; shames —		
	Writes name on board —		
			—Denies responsibility
	Accuses —		
			—Argues
Verbal steps	Feels very angry; argues — complains, blames		
			—Blames; retaliates
	Writes check on board —		
	Gives final warning —		
			—Taunts
	Threatens and challenges —		
			—Criticizes
	Argues —		
		B	
Action steps	Sends Richard to office —		
			—Disruption stops
	Makes him — write sentence		

Sharon understood where I was heading. She could see that the last few steps in her diagram were the only ones Richard regarded seriously. She was wasting her time doing things that weren't working and becoming angry in the process. My next task was to show her a way to avoid the dance.

"What would happen if you asked Richard to stop at point A then went on directly to your action steps at point B without any of these other steps in between?" I asked.

"There would be less arguing," she replied.

"Right," I agreed. "And you would be less angry. By eliminating all of these ineffective verbal steps you could stop his misbehavior with less time, energy, and upset."

Next I wanted her to see that long-term consequences actually extended the length of their power struggles. "Let's look at your action steps," I suggested. "Your action steps stop Richard's misbehavior for the moment, but they last a long time, sometimes all week. He becomes angry and resentful and takes it out on you. Then you end up doing many shorter versions of the same dance that end with threats instead of consequences."

"I don't know what else to do," she confessed. "He usually loses all of his recess privileges for the week by Monday afternoon. There isn't much left to take away, but I can't allow him to get away with it, either. He needs to know I mean business." I agreed.

"If there is a way to get that message across without making Richard angry or resentful, would you use it?" I asked.

"Of course," she replied.

"Good. Then let's put a different ending on your diagram," I suggested. "What would happen if you changed your threats to limited choices and used a time-out consequence if he persisted with his disruption? No more loss of recess time or sending him to the office. No more writing sentences or apology letters. No daily behavior reports. And no consequences at home for misbehavior at school. Your new message might sound like this: 'Richard, stop disrupting, please, and follow along quietly or you'll have to spend some quiet time by yourself. What would you like to do?'"

"It sounds so easy," laughed Sharon.

"The methods are easy compared to what you have been doing," I replied, "and you can use them with your other students as well. The hardest part will be stopping yourself from doing the dance. Richard will probably do his best to get you back out on the dance floor."

"What should I do if he argues or talks back after I give him limited choices?" asked Sharon.

"Don't take the bait," I replied. "Use the cut-off technique." I explained how it works. "If Richard really wants to discuss the matter further, arrange a time during his lunch hour or after school to do so. The time for discussion is not when your rules are being tested or violated."

"And if he persists?" she asked.

"Then follow through with a time-out so he experiences what you said," I replied. "No dance. That's a clear signal."

"Sure, I can do that," Sharon replied, eager to get started.

We spent an hour that afternoon practicing the skills she needed to end her dances. She learned how to say stop in clear and respectful terms and how to use limited choices and the cut-off technique when she encountered testing or resistance. Logical consequences and time-outs replaced the drawn-out consequences she used earlier. She explained the new plan to Richard's parents, and they agreed to put it into effect the next day. Sharon's new diagram soon looked like Figure 4F. So can yours.

Figure 4F. Sharon's new diagram

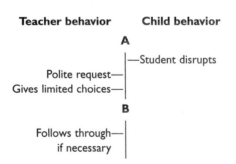

84

A Mixed Dance

Mixed dances come in various forms. Some start off punitive and end up permissive with teachers compromising their limits or giving in altogether. Others start off permissive and end up punitive when teachers react in anger and impose harsh or drawn-out consequences.

Jerry, an eighth-grade teacher, did the latter. He held the school record for sending the most students to the office in a single semester. The feat wasn't winning him many supporters. Parents were beginning to complain, and so was the school's counseling staff. One of the vice principals at his school suggested he give me a call.

"I can only take so much," Jerry complained. "The kids push me too far. That's why I send them to the office. There wouldn't be a problem if they would just cooperate and do what I ask."

He invited me to observe one of his classes and added that his fourth-period class was the worst. I agreed to observe his fourth-period class the next day. We scheduled a follow-up conference for later that afternoon.

I arrived at Jerry's fourth-period class five minutes after the bell rang and took a seat near the back of the room. The kids were curious about who I was. Several turned around to check me out.

Things were calm for the first few minutes, then the testing started. Two girls began talking and passing notes. Their talking was loud enough to disturb others, but Jerry kept on teaching as though nothing was happening. He ignored their disruption altogether. The girls continued to talk. Occasionally one giggled, then turned around and looked at me, then giggled some more. Jerry kept on teaching. Not a word was said.

When the girls saw that I wasn't going to intervene, they became bolder. They talked louder and giggled more. One of them passed a note to a boy and waited for his reaction. He read it and acted shocked, which triggered a new round of giggling. Jerry glanced in their direction several times but kept on teaching. The only change I could observe in his behavior was a slight amplification of his voice as he attempted to be heard above their chatter.

"This is interesting," I thought. "Does he eventually give them a signal?"

On the other side of the room, two boys were flicking bits of mud that had fallen off their shoes at one another. The game was great entertainment for several others nearby who chuckled each time a shot missed and nodded approval when shots were on target. Jerry seemed aware of what was going on, but not a word was said. He kept on teaching.

Finally, one of the boys did something that couldn't be ignored. He pressed a muddy shoe against the other boy's trousers and left a large print. Jerry looked at both of them impatiently.

"Come on, guys," he pleaded. "We only have thirty-five minutes to go. Can't you save the horsing around for after class?" The two settled down for the moment. Jerry returned to his teaching.

Five more minutes passed, then there was another disturbance. One of the girls who had been passing notes earlier began gesturing excitedly to the boy sitting next to her. Everyone was watching. Jerry stopped once again and looked at her impatiently.

"Jana, would you get yourself under control, please," he requested politely. "I don't want to have to ask you again." He waited for Jana to settle down. She did, and he resumed his lesson. Meanwhile the mud-flicking game started up again on the other side of the room.

Jerry looked frustrated. "How much longer can he hold out before he gives a stronger signal?" I wondered.

Jana answered my question. Without warning, she jumped up out of her seat and tried to intercept a note passed to Mark. The whole class watched as the two girls wrestled for the note. Jerry exploded.

"I've had it!" he shouted. "Jana and Shannon, you're out of here." He handed them both passes to the office. "Mark, you'll be joining them shortly if you don't settle down."

A tense silence fell over the class. Glances were exchanged, but no one disrupted. Even the mud-flicking game stopped. They knew he had reached his limit.

When I arrived for our afternoon conference, Jerry was still angry. "See what I have to put up with," he said.

"Yes," I agreed. "They pushed you pretty far. Do you usually handle disruptions the way you handled them today?" I inquired.

"Yes," he replied, "but they don't usually push me to the point where I have to send them to the office. That only happens a few times each week." Jerry was willing to overlook a lot. I wondered if he was aware of the mixed messages he sent his students. I decided to check it out.

"May I draw a diagram of the interactions I observed during your fourth-period class?" I asked. He nodded. When I finished, we both paused to look at it.

"Look familiar?" I asked.

"It sure does," he replied. "That's what I go through all day long."

"I call them classroom dances," I said. "Your dance starts off politely and ends with an angry explosion. Were you aware of all the disruptions that took place before Jana and Shannon wrestled for the note?" Jerry nodded that he was.

"When did they begin to bother you?" I asked.

"I was annoyed when Greg wiped his muddy shoe all over Randy," Jerry replied. "And I was annoyed with Jana when she made all those dramatic hand gestures and showed off for Mark. But Jana and Shannon went much too far when they started wrestling for that note. That's when I lost it."

I returned to Jerry's diagram and wrote the words "feels annoyed" after the incidents he described and the words "feels very angry" after the wrestling incident. Jerry's diagram was now complete (Figure 4G).

Figure 4G. Jerry's diagram

Teacher behavior	Child behavior
	A
	Kids disrupt (talk, pass notes)
Ignores disruption	
	Disruption continues
Continues to ignore	
	Cause more disruption
Continues to ignore	
	Boys flick mud, laughing
Feels annoyed; ignores disruption	
	Wipes muddy shoes
Pleads and cajoles	
	Pass more notes; gesture with hands
Requests cooperation	
	Continue flicking mud
Continues to ignore	
	Girls wrestle for notes
Jerry explodes; feels very angry	
	B
Sends girls to office	
	Disruption stops
Threatens Mark	

I summarized what his diagram was telling us. "The kids test you with various forms of disruption, but your first response is to ignore their misbehavior. You overlook as much as you can until you become annoyed. Then you try pleading, cajoling, and polite requests. The disruption continues. When it reaches the point where you can't take it any longer, you stop it with your action step." He nodded in agreement.

"At what point in the diagram is their disruptive behavior unacceptable to you?" I asked. He looked at me like I was crazy.

"It's never OK to disrupt," he replied.

"I agree with you, in theory," I said, "but let's look at the rule in practice. If their disruptive behavior was not OK at the beginning of the period, then why did you allow it to continue for twenty-five minutes before you finally decided to stop it?"

Jerry didn't have an answer, but he understood what I meant. He could see that he was sending a mixed message.

"Let's take a closer look at the steps in your dance," I suggested. "You use two types of steps: verbal steps and action steps. We'll include ignoring as part of your verbal steps." I drew a circle around all of his verbal steps, including the ignoring, and a box around his action steps at the very end of his diagram. "Which steps stopped the misbehavior?" I asked. He pointed to his action steps (Figure 4H).

"Exactly," I replied. "That's the first time the kids get a clear signal that you expect their disruption to stop. None of the circled steps have any lasting impact on their behavior. How do the kids know how far they can go before they've gone too far?"

"They don't know," Jerry admitted. He could see that's why they keep pushing. "How do I get out of this dance?" he asked.

Figure 4H. Jerry's verbal steps and action steps

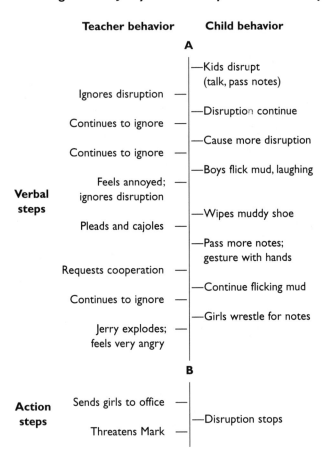

The solution is simple," I said. "Since the kids want to know how far they can go, what would happen if you gave them the information they want the first time they disrupt? Your new message might sound like this: 'You can stop disrupting or you'll have to spend some quiet time by yourself. What would you like to do?'"

"There would be much less disruption," replied Jerry, "but I still would be sending kids to the office."

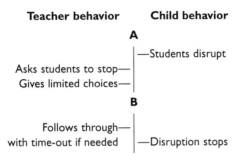

Figure 4I. Jerry's new diagram

"Then let's use a more effective action step," I suggested. I showed him how to use the two-stage time-out procedure. He introduced it to each of his classes the next day. As expected, his aggressive researchers tested it out to see if it worked. It did. They soon learned that disruptions would no longer be tolerated. Jerry's new diagram looked like the one above (Figure 4I).

Chapter Summary

Classroom dances are destructive patterns of communication and problem solving that play out over and over again when classroom rules are tested and violated. The dances come in many forms. There's a permissive version, a punitive version, and some teachers do both.

All dances begin with unclear or ineffective messages about our rules. They're fueled by anger and misunderstanding, and they all lead to escalating conflicts and power struggles. Over time, classroom dances become such a familiar and deeply ingrained habit that teachers experience them as their normal way of doing things. These teachers are not even aware that they are dancing. Awareness is the key to breaking free.

The best way to stop a classroom dance is not to start one to begin with. Teachers can avoid dances altogether by starting off with a clear verbal signal and by supporting their words with effective action. The process is easy once you discover the steps that aren't working for you. The next chapter will help you do that.

▼

Chapter

5

Are Your Limits Firm or Soft?

If you wanted to stop cars at a busy intersection, would you rely on yellow lights alone to get the job done? Not likely. Most motorists don't stop at yellow lights, and neither do children when they confront these signals in the classroom. Children don't stop for the same reason adults don't. Stopping is optional, not required.

If we really want someone to stop, we need to present the right signal: a red light. Motorists respect red lights. They associate them with consequences: collisions, tickets, and higher insurance rates. Children respond in much the same way. They're more likely to comply with our requests when we support our words with effective action.

Many teachers hold up the wrong signals to stop misbehavior in the classroom. They don't realize that their stop signs don't really require stopping or that their attempts to say no sound like yes, sometimes, or maybe to their students. The problem, in most cases, is unclear communication about limits.

Limits come in two basic varieties, soft and firm. Each conveys a different message about our rules and expectations. In this chapter, you'll discover which type of limits you use and why your students respond to you the way they do. You'll learn how to minimize the need for testing by starting off with a clear message children really understand. Let's begin by examining the messages that don't work for us. It's time to get acquainted with soft limits.

Soft Limits: When No Means Yes, Sometimes, or Maybe

Raymond, age nine, knows he's not supposed to eat snacks during class, but when his teacher isn't looking, he pulls out a bag of corn chips and starts crunching away. He's halfway through the bag before his teacher notices what's going on.

"Raymond! You know you're not supposed to eat during class," she says, with disapproval. "Put that bag away, please, and wait until lunch."

"Sorry," says Raymond, as he sticks the corn-chip bag back in his desk.

A few minutes pass before Raymond tries again. When his teacher's back is turned, he sneaks a few more chips out of the bag and chews them softly, one at a time. No one notices, so he grabs a small handful. He gets caught a second time.

"Raymond!" says his teacher with exasperation. "Are you eating chips again? I thought I told you not to." He looks apologetic. "If I let you eat during class, then I have to let everybody do it," she explains. "It's not fair to others. I really wish you would put them away and wait for lunch."

"OK," says Raymond contritely. He puts the chips back in his desk.

Raymond's teacher is using soft limits. She believes her message is getting across, but what did Raymond experience after all the reasons and explanations? It wasn't stopping. Instead, he finished most of the bag!

What did Raymond learn from this experience? He learned that eating snacks during class is really OK if he can endure his teacher's attempts to convince him not to. His teacher communicated a different message than she intended.

Soft limits are rules in theory, not in practice. They invite testing because they carry a mixed message. The verbal message seems to say stop, but the action message says that stopping is neither expected nor required. Raymond understood this clearly and responded the way most drivers do when the light turns yellow. He acknowledged his teacher's signal but continued on his way. Raymond and his teacher will likely have many more of these encounters as long as she uses soft limits.

From a training perspective, soft limits do not accomplish any of our basic goals. They don't stop misbehavior, they don't encourage acceptable behavior, and they don't promote positive learning about our rules or expectations. They simply don't work. Worse yet, they frequently achieve the opposite of their intended effect by inviting testing and power struggles. Soft limits are the cause of most classroom dances.

Soft limits come in a variety of forms. They can be ineffective verbal messages or ineffective action messages. Sometimes they are both at the same time. All share the common message that compliance is neither expected nor required. Let's look at some typical examples.

Wishes, Hopes, and Shoulds

Rhonda, age four, knows she's not supposed to use painting materials in the carpeted areas of her classroom, but both easels are in use, and she really wants to paint. She grabs a brush and a tray of paints and heads to the nearest table. Her picture is nearly complete when the teacher discovers what's going on.

"Rhonda, you know you're not supposed to use paints near the carpets. You might spill."

"I'll be careful," says Rhonda.

"I know you will," says her teacher, "but accidents can happen even when you're careful. That's why we put the easels in the tiled area. I really wish you would put the paints away and finish your picture later when an easel is free."

"OK," replies Rhonda, but she continues to paint.

Her teacher waits, but nothing happens. So she tries again. "Rhonda, do you know how difficult it is to get paint stains out of the carpet? I hope you put the paints away before there is an accident."

"I'm almost done," says Rhonda, as she dabs the brush into the blue paint jar.

"Rhonda! I'm starting to get mad," exclaims her teacher. "Is that what you want? Please do what I ask before I get even madder." Rhonda paints quickly.

Did you hear a clear message that Rhonda was required to stop painting? Rhonda didn't, and she responded the way many children do when they receive this type of mixed signal. Wishes, hopes, and shoulds are another way of saying: Stopping is nice, but you really don't have to until you're ready. Compliance is optional, not required. Often when children confront this type of signal, they test for clarification. That's what Rhonda did when she ignored her teacher and continued painting.

Repeating and Reminding

Algebra is Chad's least favorite subject. While his teacher explains equations at the board, Chad pulls out a comic book and starts reading. His teacher notices.

"Chad, I think it would be a good idea if you put that away," suggests the teacher. Chad places the comic under one of his books, then looks up attentively. As soon as his teacher returns to the lesson, Chad pulls the comic out and continues reading. Several minutes go by before he's discovered.

"Chad, how many times do I have to tell you?" asks his annoyed teacher. "Put the comic book away!"

Chad puts the comic away and waits a full fifteen minutes before he pulls it out again. This time, he conceals it under his binder and looks up periodically to give the impression he's paying attention. His teacher isn't fooled. He walks over to Chad's desk and lifts up the binder.

"That's enough!" says the teacher. "Put the comic in your backpack or you can give it to me and pick it up after school." Chad puts the comic in his backpack.

When Chad ignored the first request, nothing happened, so he decided to test and try again. The second request followed the same pattern. If the teacher did not mean what he said the first two times, why should Chad take his words seriously the third time? He doesn't.

Teachers who repeat and remind are teaching kids to ignore and tune out. Like many students who wonder how far they can go, Chad doesn't comply with his teacher's request until he has to.

Speeches, Lectures, and Sermons

Robin, a fifth grader, strolls into class five minutes late from recess. "Where have you been, Robin?" asks her annoyed teacher. "The bell rang nearly five minutes ago."

"I had to use the restroom," Robin replies.

"You need to take care of bathroom trips before the bell rings," admonishes her teacher. "I don't appreciate your lack of consideration. I've already given directions for the next assignment, and now I have to repeat them just for you. You're holding everybody up. What kind of a class

97

would this be if everyone showed up when they felt like it? It isn't fair. Now, take your seat, please, so we can started."

Did you hear a clear message that showing up late would not be tolerated? Robin didn't. Will the lecture help her arrive on time in the future? Probably not.

What did Robin learn from all of this? She learned that showing up late is really OK if she can tolerate her teacher's lectures. This is not a bad deal for someone who wants to avoid classwork and extend recess time. Robin knows from experience that she can count on her teacher to provide a set of personal instructions when she arrives late.

Warnings and Second Chances

It's a sunny day, and Mrs. Adams decides to take her second graders outside and read them a story. When everyone is seated, she begins. Within minutes, several students begin horsing around.

"Dale and Ernie, would you like to sit together?" asks Mrs. Adams. They both nod. "Then you will have to follow along quietly. That's a warning."

She resumes her story. A few moments later, the boys poke and tickle each other again. Mrs. Adams puts her book down. "Guys, didn't I ask you to follow along quietly?" she asks. They both nod. "Well, I meant it, too. This is your final warning." She returns to her story.

This time, things are quiet for a full five minutes, then Ernie lets out a yelp. "He pinched me!" complains Ernie.

"It was an accident," says Dale.

Mrs. Adams isn't sure what happened. "OK, this is your last chance," she says. "If I hear any more disruptions, I'm going to separate you. Do you understand?" The boys nod. She resumes her story.

Do you think she has seen the last of their disruptions? Not likely. The boys violated her rule three times, and each time they received a warning and another chance.

They'll probably continue to test until they receive a signal that requires stopping.

Cooperate, OK?

Three-year-old Shelly knows she's supposed to put her materials away when she's done with them, but she leaves her completed puzzle on the floor and begins playing in the sand trays. Her teacher notices.

"Shelly, you left your puzzle on the floor," says the teacher. "You're supposed to put it away before you begin something new. OK?"

Shelly acknowledges her teacher's words but continues to play with the sand trays. Her teacher tries again. "Shelly, if everybody left their projects laying around, our classroom would be a mess. Please pick up the puzzle and put it away, OK?" This time, Shelly doesn't even look up.

What does it mean when we ask a child to do something, then add "OK?" at the end of our request? OK with whom? The child? Or the teacher? What happens if it's not OK with the child? Does that mean cooperation is optional? And who decides? Shelly seems to have made up her mind. When we add "OK?" to the end of our requests, we obscure the clarity of our message.

Statements of Fact

The sixth-period bell rings, and Mr. Gilbert moves to the front of the class to begin his lesson. He's ready, but many of his students are not. They talk and joke around. Several haven't even made it to their seats. Mr. Gilbert waits patiently.

"I'm ready to start," he announces, but his words have little impact. The kids continue to talk. Mr. Gilbert waits a little longer. "I can't get started until it's quiet," he says. The talking continues. Mr. Gilbert is angry.

Did you hear that the students were required to stop talking and get in their seats? Neither did they. Many continued to test for that message. Mr. Gilbert is not likely to get the cooperation he expects until he gives a clearer signal. Statements of fact do not convey the intended message.

Ignoring the Misbehavior

Lyle, a sixth grader, enjoys being the class clown. Each day, he pulls a series of gags and stunts to amuse his classmates. His teacher is not amused. She finds his behavior irritating and tries to ignore it in the hope that it will go away. She encourages his classmates to ignore him, too, but Lyle shows no sign of slowing down.

Is the absence of a green light the same as a red light? If it was, Lyle would have stopped his clowning long ago. When we ignore misbehavior, we are really saying: It's OK to do that. Go ahead. You don't have to stop. That's the message Lyle follows.

If Lyle's teacher wants to stop his clowning, she needs to give him the right signal. She needs to say stop with her words, and, if needed, follow through with her actions by temporarily removing Lyle from his audience. Lyle will learn his teacher's rule when he experiences the consequences of his unacceptable behavior.

Reasoning and Explaining

A group of fourth-grade boys have invented a variation of the game of tag. When someone is tagged, the tagger yells out for the others to pile on the new person who becomes "it." The game is great fun, but not very safe. When the yard-duty teacher sees what's happening, he intervenes.

"Guys, that game doesn't look safe. Someone could get hurt. You can play tag without piling on."

"Come on, Mr. Kearney," pleads one boy. "No one is going to get hurt. We'll be careful."

"I know you will," replies Mr. Kearney, "but the blacktop is hard, and Nick could have been hurt when you guys piled on him. I'm concerned."

"But Nick didn't mind," says one boy. "Yeah, he liked it," says another. Nick nods in agreement.

"Well, it's still not a good idea," says Mr. Kearney, "It's best that you stop."

The boys grumble a little but head off. A few minutes pass, then Mr. Kearney hears, "Pile on Jared!" This time, he sees the same group of boys piling on Jared. Mr. Kearney calls them over.

"Guys, didn't I ask you not to do that?"

"You said it wasn't OK on the blacktop," says one boy. "We're on the grass. It's safe here."

"Piling on is not safe anywhere," insists Mr. Kearney. "Someone might get hurt. You guys would feel terrible if that happened, and so would I. That's why we don't allow rough games on the playground. They lead to problems. Do you understand?"

The boys nod and head off once again. This time, they select an area well away from Mr. Kearney before they resume the game. Mr. Kearney decides to check it out. Sure enough, the boys are at it again. He calls them over.

"Guys, you don't seem to understand what I've been trying to tell you," says a frustrated Mr. Kearney. "That game is dangerous. I'm not going to wait for someone to get hurt before it stops. If I see any of you piling on again, you'll spend the rest of your recess on the bench." No one wants to spend their recess on the bench. The game stops.

Mr. Kearney believes he said stop each time he gave reasons and explanations about the dangers of piling on, but what did the boys experience? They didn't stop. Cooperation was optional, not required. The boys knew it and continued to pile on until they experienced a signal that required them to stop.

Is there a time for giving reasons and explanations? Yes, but that time is not when our rules are being tested or violated. When children test or go too far, they need to know the consequences of their behavior. Reasons and explanations do not provide them with the data they need to complete their research.

Bargaining and Negotiating

Lynn, a high-school sophomore, knows she's supposed to turn in her biography assignment on Wednesday, but it's Monday, and she hasn't even started. She asks for a deadline extension.

"Mr. Edwards, may I have a few extra days to complete my biography assignment?" Lynn asks.

"You've had three weeks," says Mr. Edwards. "That should have been plenty of time for a project under ten pages."

"I know, but it's taking longer than I expected. May I turn it in on Monday?" she asks.

"No, but you can turn it in on Friday for full credit," he replies.

"Oh, please! Mr. Edwards," Lynn pleads. "I'll do a better job if I can have a few more days. May I have the weekend, please?"

"OK," concedes Mr. Edwards, frustrated by his weakening position, "but just this once. Next time, you'll have to finish on time like everybody else."

Did you hear that getting assignments in on time was expected and required? Lynn didn't. Her teacher was willing to bargain and negotiate about the due date for the assignment. In effect, Mr. Edwards is saying: "My rules are negotiable. Let's make a deal." Lynn tested to see how far she could go.

To children, negotiable feels a lot like optional. By the time the negotiation session is over, Lynn understands the real rule is "Complete your assignments on time unless you can talk your way out of it." Teachers who bargain and negotiate over their rules invite children to test and redefine those rules.

Arguing and Debating

Terry, a second grader, knows he's supposed to clean around his desk before he leaves in the afternoon, but he tries to sneak out the door unnoticed. His teacher calls him back. "Terry, you can't leave until you pick up around your desk and put your books and papers away," she says.

"I don't see why I have to clean up when Shelton doesn't," says Terry.

"Shelton's desk is clean, and he put his books away," replies the teacher. "That's what you need to do, too."

"Well, it didn't look that way yesterday," argues Terry, "and you let him go. It's not fair."

"We're not talking about Shelton," replies his teacher. "We're talking about you, and you know what you have to do."

"You're not fair," Terry complains, looking for a little bargaining room. "Why do I have to do things others don't have to do?"

"I'll keep a closer eye on Shelton's desk from now on," says the teacher, "and I'll make sure he follows the rules just like you."

"Well, they're stupid rules!" says Terry.

"Stupid or not, they won't change all year," says the teacher. She walks to her desk and begins to correct papers. When Terry realizes that he can't talk his way out of it, he heads over to clean up his desk.

What was not happening while the arguing and debating was going on? Of course, Terry was not cleaning up his desk. That won't happen until the argument is over. Some arguments can last a long time.

What is the message Terry's teacher sends by arguing and debating over her rules? Isn't she saying that her rules are subject to further discussion and debate? That's what Terry thinks. She invited resistance and a power struggle by allowing Terry to test her limits and prolong his resistance.

Pleading and Cajoling

It's snack time, and four-year-old Trent decides to amuse his friends by spitting gobs of chocolate pudding on the table. "Ooh, gross!" says the girl sitting next to him, but Trent keeps it up. *Plop.* Another gob hits the table. His teacher intervenes.

"Come on, Trent," she says. "It's not nice to eat like that. The kids think you're gross. Show me you can eat like a big boy." The words barely leave her lips when the next gob hits the table. *Plop.* Trent smiles mischievously.

"OK, Trent, you've had your fun. Now, let's eat the right way, OK?" she pleads. But Trent is having a ball. He spits out two more gobs. "You usually have such good table manners," she says. "We all would feel better if you stopped that."

Did Trent hear a message that stopping was expected and required? No. He heard a lot of pleading and cajoling and a message that said it would be nice if he stopped. Trent thinks it would be nice if he doesn't. If Trent's teacher really wants him to stop, she needs to say stop clearly with her words and remove the pudding if he doesn't. Without a clear signal, he's not likely to give up his game.

Bribes and Special Rewards

Every day Mr. Sawyer complains in the staff lounge about one of his disruptive fifth graders. "Why don't you offer him some special rewards for better classroom behavior," suggests a well-meaning colleague. "Maybe you can buy his cooperation."

Mr. Sawyer is desperate. He decides to give it a try. The next day after school, he calls Carl to his desk and asks about the things Carl enjoys most. Carl shares the typical list—pizza, ice cream, video games, baseball cards, skateboarding, and street hockey.

"How would you like to earn a pack of baseball cards every day at school?" Mr. Sawyer asks. Carl perks up. "All you need to do is complete a whole day without disrupting class," says Mr. Sawyer. "Do we have a deal?" Carl nods.

The agreement resulted in a dramatic turnaround in Carl's behavior. He earned four packs of cards the first week and five packs during weeks two and three. Carl liked the new arrangement, but Mr. Sawyer was having second thoughts. By the end of the third week, he had paid out nearly twenty dollars. Carl's cooperation was expensive.

"None of my other students have to be paid to cooperate," Mr. Sawyer thinks to himself. "Carl has already shown that he can do it. I shouldn't have to pay him any longer." The more he thinks about it, the madder he becomes. He decides to revise the terms of their agreement.

When Carl came up to collect his cards the next day, Mr. Sawyer says, "Carl, I don't think we need to do this anymore. You've shown that you know how to cooperate."

"No way!" says Carl. "I'm not doing it unless you give me the cards." Carl's cooperation stopped as soon as the reward was withheld.

When we offer children bribes and special rewards in return for cooperation, aren't we really saying with our actions that we don't expect them to cooperate unless we pay them off? That's what Carl thought. Bribes and special rewards are another form of soft limits.

Unclear Directions

Mrs. Robie, a seventh-grade teacher, selects two students to return an overhead projector to the school's equipment room. She suspects they may try to stretch the trip out longer than it should be. "Don't take too long," she says, as they leave the room. "I want you back on time."

What does "too long" mean to a couple of seventh graders who enjoy being out of class? Five minutes? Ten minutes? Fifteen minutes? And who decides? Isn't Mrs. Robie making an assumption that she and her students share the same belief about how long the trip should take?

Unclear or open-ended directions invite testing and set up both students and teacher for conflict. If Mrs. Robie expects the students back in five minutes, she should say, "I expect you back in five minutes."

Ineffective Role Modeling

Mr. Allen, a high-school teacher, sees two boys in the hallway yelling, threatening, and calling each other names. They're squared off and ready to fight. He intervenes.

"Knock it off!" he shouts, as he pushes the boys apart. "You're both acting like a couple of jerks. If you want to make fools out of yourselves, do it on your own time. Now, get to class before I send you to the office!" Reluctantly, the boys head their separate ways.

What did the boys learn from this encounter? They attempted to resolve their conflict with yelling, threatening, and name-calling. What did Mr. Allen do? He resolved the conflict with yelling, threatening, and name-calling. In effect, he was teaching them to do the very thing he was reprimanding them for.

Inconsistency Between the Classroom and the Office

There are two minutes until recess, and Jamie, a second grader, has art supplies spread out all over her desk.

"You can't go out for recess until you put your art supplies away," says the teacher, as she passes by Jamie's desk. Jamie tries to bargain her way out of it.

"If I do it now, I'll be the last one in line for hopscotch. Why can't I do it after recess?" Jamie pleads. Her teacher holds firm. When the bell rings, Jamie tries to sneak out. Her teacher intercepts her at the door.

"Not so fast, Jamie," says the teacher. "First, you need to put your things away."

"I won't do it!" says Jamie defiantly.

"That's up to you, but you can't leave for recess until you do," says the teacher.

"I still won't do it," says Jamie.

Her teacher is not about to spend her break period arguing with Jamie. She gives Jamie some choices.

"You can clean it up now or work the problem out with Mr. Thompkins, our principal, if you prefer," says the teacher. She escorts Jamie to the office and explains the situation to Mr. Thompkins.

When she's done, Mr. Thompkins calls Jamie into his office and listens to her side of the story. "I don't see what difference it makes if she picks up before or after recess," Mr. Thompkins thinks to himself. He decides to let her off the hook. "OK, this time, I'll let you go out to play, but it's important to cooperate with your teacher. Now, run along."

What did Jamie learn? In effect, there are two sets of rules operating: the teacher's rules that say pick up your mess before you can go out to play and the principal's rules that say you don't have to if you have a good reason not to. Which set of rules will prevail?

What do you think Jamie will say next time her teacher wants her to pick something up before recess? Sure, she'll probably play the principal against the teacher by saying, "Mr. Thompkins says I don't have to do it."

If Mr. Thompkins decides to hold firm next time, Jamie will probably say, "Last time you said that I didn't have to do it." Inconsistency between the classroom and the office sets up Jamie for testing and all three for conflict.

More Examples of Ineffective Verbal Messages (Soft Limits)

"Would you cooperate just once in a while?"

"Come on, get your act together!"

"Would you do me a favor and pay attention?"

"Can't you see I'm trying to teach a lesson?"

"Would you yell a little softer?"

"You better shape up."

"I don't care for your attitude."

"I don't believe it. You actually did what I asked."

"Would you like it if I interrupted you?"

"Stop acting like a jerk!"

"Is it asking too much to have a little cooperation?"

"I've had enough from you!"

More Examples of Ineffective Action Messages (Soft Limits)

Allowing students to walk away from a mess.

Cleaning up students' messes for them.

Overlooking misbehavior when you're in a good mood.

Overlooking misbehavior to avoid embarrassment.

Giving in to persistent nagging.

Giving in to a tantrum.

Firm Limits: When No Really Means No

Artie, a kindergartner, thinks it's funny to wipe finger paint on Selena, the girl who sits next to him. Selena doesn't share his humor. When he touches her, she complains.

"Artie, keep your hands away from Selena," says the teacher. "If you do that again, you'll have to put your picture away and sit by yourself for a while. Is that clear?"

Artie nods, but as soon as the teacher walks away, he reaches over and wipes a gooey streak of fingerpaint all over Selena's arm.

"He did it again!" complains Selena.

"It's time to clean up, Artie," says his teacher matter-of-factly. She helps him up from his seat and leads him over to the sink. "You can draw quietly at the back table until the others finish." No shaming or blaming. No disapproving lectures or negative attention.

Artie's teacher is using firm limits to teach her rule. Her words say stop and so do her actions when she separates Artie from the others. Artie has all the information he needs to make a more acceptable choice next time he's tempted to wipe finger paint on a classmate.

Firm limits send clear signals about our rules and expectations. Children understand that we mean what we say and learn to take our words seriously. The result—less testing, better communication, and no classroom dances. Firm limits are effective teaching tools.

Guidelines for Using Firm Limits

Effective guidance begins with a clear message with our words. Most often that's where communication breaks down. The following tips will help you improve the quality of your verbal messages.

1. *Keep the focus of your message on behavior.*

Keep the focus of your message on what you want the child to do or stop doing, not on attitude or feelings or the worth of the child. Remember, our goal is to reject unacceptable behavior, not the child performing the behavior. A clear behavioral message is less likely to be perceived as a personal attack.

For example, if you want Sharon, a tenth grader, to stop talking during your lesson, your message should be "Sharon you can talk with your friends during lunch or after class but not now." Your message should not be "Sharon, do you have to be so annoying?" or "Why are you being so rude?" or "Would you like it if I interrupted you while you were trying to teach?"

2. *Be direct and specific.*

A firm limit-setting message should inform children, directly and specifically, about what you want them to do. If necessary, be prepared to tell them how and when you want them to do it.

For example, if you want Kyle, age nine, to clean up his desk before he leaves for home, your message should be "Kyle, pick up thoroughly around your desk before you leave. That means picking up all the crayons, pencils, or any other items that are on the floor, and putting away all your books and papers. If that's not done, you won't be ready to go."

Avoid indirect unclear messages such as "I hope you do a better job picking up around your desk today." What is "a better job"? And who decides? You or Kyle? What happens if your definition is different from his? Without a direct and specific message, Kyle's performance will probably fall short of your expectations.

3. *Use your normal voice.*

The tone of your voice is important. Your normal voice expresses control whereas your raised voice sends the opposite message—loss of control. Firm limits are not stated harshly. There is no need to raise your voice to convince children that you really mean what you say. Your actions will convey your resolve more powerfully than words.

4. *Specify your consequences if necessary.*

If you expect testing or noncompliance, then specify the consequences for noncompliance at the same time you make your request. This is not a threat. You are just giving your aggressive researchers all the data they need to make an acceptable choice.

For example, if you ask Larry, a second grader, to put away his Silly Putty during class, but you expect him to test, your message should be "Larry, put away the Silly Putty, please. If you have it out during class again, I'll have to keep it in my desk until the next parent-teacher conference."

Now, Larry has all the information he needs to make an acceptable choice. He may still decide to test, but if he does, all you have to do is follow through with your action step and take the Silly Putty away. Larry will learn you mean what you say.

5. *Support your words with effective action.*

Your words are only the first part of your total message. In many cases, your words will be all you'll need, but even the clearest verbal message will be ineffective if you fail to support your words with effective action. Be prepared to follow through.

111

Examples of Effective Verbal
Messages (Firm Limits)

"Stop pushing now."

"It's not OK to interrupt."

"I expect you back in five minutes."

"If you wipe the glue stick on others, I'll have to take it away."

"You can play by the rules or find another game to play."

"If you shove, you'll have to go to the back of the line."

"You won't be ready to leave until your desk is clean."

Examples of Effective Action
Messages (Firm Limits)

Using a time-out consequence for persistent disruption.

Removing a toy from a child who does not put it away when asked.

Revoking a play privilege temporarily for failing to play by the rules.

Separating a child from others for misbehaving in the cafeteria.

Temporary loss of a privilege for abusing that privilege.

Holding students accountable for cleaning up their messes.

Summary

Limits are signals that communicate important messages. They convey our rules and expectations. They help children conduct their research, and they define the balance of power and authority in teacher-student relationships.

Limits come in two basic varieties, firm and soft (Figure 5A). Soft limits are rules in theory, not in practice.

Figure 5A. Comparison of firm and soft limits

	Firm limits	Soft limits
Characteristics	Stated in clear, direct, concrete behavioral terms.	Stated in unclear terms or as mixed messages.
	Words supported by actions.	Actions do not support intended rule.
	Compliance expected and required.	Compliance optional; not required.
	Provide information needed to make acceptable choices and cooperate.	Do not provide information needed to make acceptable choices.
	Provide accountability.	Lack accountability.
Predictable outcomes	Cooperation.	Resistance.
	Decreased limit testing.	Increased limit testing.
	Clear understanding of rules and expectations.	Escalating misbehavior, power struggles.
	Regard teacher's words seriously.	Ignore and tune out teacher's words.
Children learn	No means no.	No means yes, sometimes, or maybe.
	"I'm expected and required to follow the rules."	"I'm not expected to follow rules."
	"Rules apply to me like everyone else."	"Rules are for others, not me."
	"I am responsible for my own behavior."	"I make my own rules and do what I want."
	Adults mean what they say.	Adults don't mean what they say.
		"Adults are responsible for my behavior."

These ineffective teaching tools contribute to miscommunication and testing as children attempt to clarify what we mean. Soft limits take many forms. They can be ineffective verbal messages or ineffective action messages. Sometimes they are both. All soft limits are mixed messages that invite power struggles and dances.

In contrast, firm limits are highly effective teaching tools. They send clear signals about our rules and expectations and help children do their research. Children trained with firm limits test less often because they understand that compliance is both expected and required.

6

Stopping Power Struggles Before They Begin

If tuning out was an Olympic event, nine-year-old Travis would be a gold medal contender. He knows how to ignore directions better than any student in his class, and he can hook almost any teacher into a power struggle. Once he hooks them, he's a master at wearing them down with arguments and debates. Travis has perfected his skills with years of practice at home.

What Travis doesn't realize is that his current teacher has figured out his game. She read a book about classroom dances and recognizes his tactics for what they are. She's ready to stop his dances before they begin. She gets her chance the next day.

When Travis is supposed to be working at his seat, he gets up, walks to the back of the room, and turns on the computer. Then he begins playing a game.

"Travis, you need to finish your paragraphs before you're ready for computer time," says his teacher. Travis doesn't respond. He continues playing.

"She'll remind me a few more times," he says to himself, "then she'll get upset and give me a final warning before I have to return to my seat. I'll probably get a full game in."

Not this time. His teacher walks over to the computer. "Travis, what did I ask you to do?" she inquires matter-of-factly.

Travis is dumbfounded. "What is going on?" he wonders. "No reminders or upset? No final warnings or instructions?" He can't believe it. She places her hand on the keyboard and waits for his response.

"You said I need to finish my paragraphs before any computer time," he replies.

"Right," she says, with her hand still on the keyboard. "Now do it, please."

But Travis isn't ready to give up so easily. He tries a different tactic. "I don't see why I can't finish the game I've already started," he says, looking for a little bargaining room. He presents the bait skillfully, but his teacher doesn't bite.

"We're done talking about it, Travis," she says matter-of-factly. "If you bring it up again, the computer won't be available to you for the rest of the day. If you really want to know why you can't use the computer now, we can arrange a time to discuss it after school or during one of your recesses." Travis doesn't want to know why that bad. He heads back to his seat to finish up.

As the example illustrates, the best way to stop a classroom dance is not to start one. We need to begin with a clear verbal message and be prepared to move quickly to our action step if needed. Travis's teacher does this effectively. You can, too, but if you've danced in the past, don't expect your students to give up their testing quickly.

Your aggressive researchers will likely challenge even your clearest verbal messages and do everything they can to get you back out on the dance floor. You'll probably be tempted to go along with it, too. Resist the temptation. The three techniques in this chapter will help you interrupt your dances before they begin.

The Check-In Procedure

When we give a clear message with our words, but students don't respond as expected, sometimes we're not sure if our message was heard or understood. We wonder: "Did my message get across? Am I being ignored? Is it time to move on to my action step?"

The check-in procedure is a simple technique that helps us answer these questions without getting hooked into the old repeating and reminding routine. When in doubt, check in with the child by saying one of the following:

"What did I ask you to do?"

"Did you understand what I said?"

"Were my directions clear?"

"Tell me in your words what you heard me say."

For example, morning snack is over, and it's time for Mrs. Jansen's preschoolers to get ready to go out to the playground. "Put your napkins, wrappers, and other garbage in the waste can," she says. Most of them do, except for Stacey who just looks at her blankly, then heads to the door with her classmates.

"Did she hear what I said?" wonders Mrs. Jansen. "She doesn't act like she did." Mrs. Jansen is tempted to ask Stacey a second time when she remembers the technique

117

she learned in the book—when in doubt, use the check-in procedure. She gives it a try.

"Stacey, what did I ask you to do before you go outside?" asks Mrs. Jansen.

"Pick up my mess," replies Stacey.

"Then do it, please," says Mrs. Jansen matter-of-factly. Stacey goes back to pick up her mess.

In this case, Stacey was limit testing. She had the information she needed but chose to ignore it. She fully expected to hear a lot of repeating and reminding before she would actually have to pick up her mess, if she would have to pick it up at all. The check-in procedure helped her teacher to clarify their communication, avoid a dance, and eliminate the payoffs for tuning out all at the same time (Figure 6A).

Now, let's consider another scenario. Let's say that when Mrs. Jansen checks in with Stacey, she responds with the same blank stare because she really was tuned out completely. What should Mrs. Jansen do?

She should give Stacey the information that Stacey missed the first time and preview her action step. Mrs.

Figure 6A. The check-in procedure

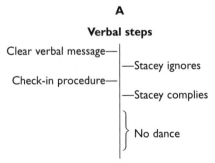

Teacher behavior	Child behavior
A	
Verbal steps	
Clear verbal message—	
	—Stacey ignores
Check-in procedure—	
	—Stacey complies
	No dance

Jansen's message might sound like this: "Put your napkins, wrappers, and other garbage away before you go outside. You won't be ready to leave until that job is done." Now Stacey has all the information she needs to make an acceptable choice. All Mrs. Jansen needs to do is follow through.

The check-in procedure also can be used in situations where children respond to our requests with mixed messages; that is, they give us the right verbal response but continue to do what they want. Sam, a high-school senior, is an expert at this. He sits in his seventh-period literature class and doodles when he's supposed to be writing a short plot summary. There are thirty minutes left in the period. The teacher notices his lack of progress.

"Sam, you have thirty minutes to finish up," he says as he passes by Sam's desk.

"I will," says Sam, but ten minutes go by, and he hasn't written a sentence. He hopes to avoid the assignment altogether or talk his way out of it when the bell rings. His teacher suspects this also and decides to check-in.

"Sam, what did I ask you to do?" inquires his teacher.

"I'll finish up," says Sam in a reassuring voice.

The teacher clarifies Sam's message. "Your words say that you will, but your actions say you won't. Let me be more clear. You won't be ready to leave until you finish your plot summary. I'll be happy to stay with you after school if you need more time to finish up." Now his teacher's message is very clear.

"Darn! It didn't work," Sam says to himself. He gets out a clean piece of paper and hurries to complete the assignment before the bell rings.

The Cut-Off Technique

The cut-off technique is an effective method for interrupting dances when children try to hook us into arguing, debating, bargaining, or compromising our limits. As the name implies, the cut-off ends the interaction by specifying a consequence if it continues. The "Or what?" question is answered. If children continue testing, follow through with your consequence. Either way, the dance stops, and your students receive the clear message they need.

When children try to engage you in arguments, debates, bargaining, or other forms of verbal sparring, say one of the following:

> "We're done talking about it. If you bring it up again, then . . ." (Follow through with your action step.)

> "Discussion time is over. You can do what you were asked, or you can spend some quiet time by yourself getting ready to do it. What would you like to do?" (Follow through with a time-out consequence.)

For example, a group of sixth-grade boys play catch with a football on the blacktop area. Their errant passes barely miss younger children playing nearby. The yard-duty teacher intervenes.

"Guys, it's not OK to play catch on the blacktop," says the teacher matter-of-factly. "You can play on the grass away from the younger children."

"We're not hurting anybody," says one boy.

"Why can't they move if they don't want to get hurt?" asks another.

The teacher isn't sure his message got across. He decides to check in. "Did you guys understand what I asked you to do?" he inquires.

"Yeah, but I don't see why we should," says one boy. The others nod in agreement.

"I'm not going to debate with them about why they should follow the rules," the teacher thinks to himself. He decides to end this potential power struggle before it begins. "We're done talking about it," he says. "If you pass the ball on the blacktop again, I'll have to take it away, and you'll spend the rest of the recess on the bench."

Now his message is really clear. The boys know their options. They have all the information they need to make an acceptable decision. Whether they cooperate or test, either way, they will learn the rule he's trying to teach. No dances this time (Figure 6B).

Emily's first-period teacher also uses the cut-off technique effectively when Emily arrives late to class and tries to talk her way out of a tardy slip.

"I was only a couple of minutes late, Miss Stevens," pleads Emily. "It won't happen again. I promise."

"I hope not," replies Miss Stevens "but you still need to pick up a tardy slip before I can let you back in class."

"It's not fair!" insists Emily, hoping for a little bargaining room. It nearly works. Miss Stevens is about to argue

Figure 6B. The cut-off technique

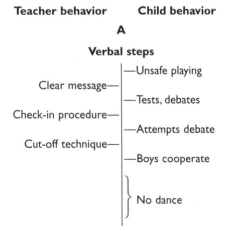

121

the issue of fairness when she remembers the technique she read about in the book.

"We're done talking about it, Emily," says Miss Stevens matter-of-factly. "If you want to discuss it further, we can arrange a time with your counselor after you pick up your tardy slip." That wasn't what Emily wanted to hear. Reluctantly, she heads to the attendance office.

The Cooldown

Effective problem solving is difficult for anyone to do, adults or children, in an atmosphere of anger and frustration. The cooldown is an excellent method for restoring self-control and stopping angry dances before they begin. This method keeps both sides off the dance floor until the time is right for problem solving. The procedure is easy to carry out. In situations of anger or upset, separate yourself from the child by saying one of the following:

When both sides are upset "I think we both need a little time to cool down. Have a seat at the back table. We'll talk about it during our next break."

When the child is upset "You look angry to me. You can cool down at the back table or in Mrs. Kenner's classroom next door. What would you like to do?"

When the teacher is upset "I'm feeling angry, and I need some time to cool down. You can read quietly at your desk while I get myself under control or you can put your head down for five minutes."

Be sure to allow sufficient time for all parties to restore control before attempting further problem solving. Don't assume the child has calmed down because you have. If communication breaks down a second time, use the procedure again. Use it as often as you need it. The following example illustrates how it works.

Brett, age nine, lives in a home where discipline involves a lot of yelling, name-calling, threats, and angry accusations. Often he arrives at school upset and on the defensive. Even minor corrections can set him off. That's what happened when his teacher tried to refocus him during a math exercise.

"Brett, turn around in your seat, please," says the teacher matter-of-factly. "You only have ten minutes to finish the worksheet."

"Why don't you say something to Greg!" shouts Brett. "He talked to me first. Why do I always get blamed?" Brett's face is flushed with anger, but his teacher knows what to do.

"Brett, you look pretty angry," she says in a calm voice. "I'll set the timer for five minutes. Take some time to cool down."

Brett picks up his pencil and worksheet and heads to their prearranged cooldown area at the back table. He grumbles and complains the whole way there, but the five minutes helps. When the timer goes off, he's under control and ready to rejoin the class. No angry dances this time. Brett is learning a tool for managing his angry feelings.

Sometimes teachers need time to cool down more than their students. That's what Mr. Conner discovered when he became a junior-high-school teacher. His quick temper caused of a lot of angry dances. He was wearing down when one of his colleagues suggested he give me a call.

"The kids know my buttons," Mr. Conner confessed. "They push the hardest when they know I'm close to losing it. I think they enjoy watching me blow up."

I asked him to describe what his students did to push his buttons. Then I asked him to describe, from beginning to end, what he did in response to their behavior. As

Figure 6C. Mr. Conner's diagram

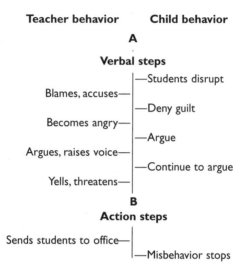

Teacher behavior   Child behavior

A

Verbal steps

　　　　　　　　　　　　—Students disrupt

Blames, accuses—

　　　　　　　　　　　　—Deny guilt

Becomes angry—

　　　　　　　　　　　　—Argue

Argues, raises voice—

　　　　　　　　　　　　—Continue to argue

Yells, threatens—

B

Action steps

Sends students to office—

　　　　　　　　　　　　—Misbehavior stops

he spoke, I diagrammed the interaction on the board (Figure 6C).

Mr. Conner's diagram revealed an angry, punitive dance. The dance usually began with a minor disruption, and Mr. Conner usually responded with blaming and accusations. When his students denied their guilt or attempted to argue, which they usually did, he became angry and raised his voice. The more they argued, the angrier he became. Before he knew it, he was shouting and threatening to send them to the office. It was clear from Mr. Conner's diagram that he didn't know how to stop his dances short of an angry explosion. He needed a way to restore self-control before things went too far.

I showed him how to start off with a clear message and how to use the cut-off technique and time-out procedure when students tried to hook him into arguments. Now he was prepared to interrupt his dances, but he still needed a tool to restore his self-control. I introduced the cooldown

Figure 6D. **The cooldown**

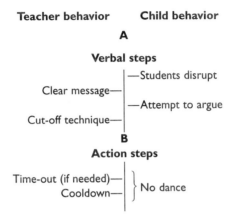

and encouraged him to use it whenever he felt hot. We arranged a follow-up conference two weeks later.

"How did it go?" I asked when Mr. Conner arrived for our follow-up. He looked more relaxed.

"The methods worked!" he said. "When my students try to hook me into arguments, I tell them we're done talking about it and send them to the classroom next door for a time-out if they persist. If I feel hot, I take out a book and read quietly for five minutes, and I ask my students to do the same. No yelling. No threats. No shouting. The kids know things are different. They don't try to push my buttons as often." Mr. Conner had some new tools for stopping his dances and staying under control. His new diagram looked like Figure 6D.

Summary

In this chapter, we examined three effective techniques for interrupting dances before they begin. When kids ignore or tune out, use the check-in procedure. When kids try to wear you down with nagging, arguments, or debates, use the cut-off technique. Finally, when kids respond to your requests with anger or when you're on the brink of losing control yourself, use the cooldown. The best way to stop a classroom dance is not to start one.

7

Positive Ways to Motivate

Limits define the path we want students to stay on, but limits alone may not motivate them to head in the intended direction. Cooperation is still a voluntary act. Short of using consequences, what can we do to inspire their cooperation? How can we tip the scales in our favor?

This chapter will show you how to do that. You'll learn how to inspire children's cooperation through the power of encouragement. The methods are quick, effective, and inexpensive in terms of not draining your time and energy. You'll find them a refreshing alternative to punishment and coercion.

Motivation and Limit Setting

Imagine two different paths in front of you. One involves only work, and the teacher uses a lot of criticism, threats, and coercion to keep you on it. The other mixes work with pleasure, and the teacher uses a lot of encouragement and respectful guidance to keep you on it. Which path would you choose? Of course, the choice is clear.

The question illustrates a basic truth that applies to all of us, children included. The more positives we see in our path, the more likely we are to head in the intended direction. A path with positives is always most inviting.

When it comes to motivating children, most teachers head in one of two directions. They take a positive approach and use generous helpings of encouragement and rewards to inspire the behavior they want. Or they take a negative approach and rely primarily on threats, punishment, and coercion to force children into cooperating. There isn't much in between.

The approach teachers use has a lot to do with the type of limits they set. Teachers who are ineffective in their limit setting are accustomed to encountering resistance. They get angry and frustrated, and often they end up saying discouraging things to their students. They assume that the problem is their students' lack of cooperation, not the way cooperation is being requested. Discouraging messages and ineffective limits go hand in hand.

Teachers who use firm limits, on the other hand, expect cooperation, but they recognize that children are most likely to cooperate when asked in a respectful manner. Encouraging messages inspire cooperation. Firm limits and encouraging messages also go hand in hand.

Encouraging and discouraging messages have different effects on children's behavior. One leads to cooperation. The other leads predictably to resistance. If our goal is to inspire cooperation, then discouraging messages are one of the surest ways not to achieve our objective.

Discouraging Messages Inspire Resistance

It's nine o'clock in the morning, and Tyler, a fifth grader, has already disrupted the class three times. Number four is about to happen. He chips a piece off the end of his eraser and flicks it at the girl sitting across from him. He gets the expected response.

"Cut it out! Tyler," she complains, loud enough for the teacher to hear.

"What does it take to get through to you, Tyler?" says his exasperated teacher. "Can't you see others don't appreciate your clowning around? I expect your behavior from a first grader, but not a fifth grader. Why don't you act your age for a change?"

"Why don't you try to be an interesting teacher for a change?" says Tyler. He knows she's hooked. Things are about to escalate.

"Nobody talks to me like that!" his teacher explodes. "I've had enough of your disrespect. You may think that you can treat people like dirt, but you'll end up tasting your own medicine." She hands Tyler two sheets of paper and directs him to the back table. "You can return to your desk after you write one hundred times: I will not be disrespectful to my teacher."

"No way!" says Tyler defiantly. "You can't make me if I don't want to."

"You can't go out for any recesses until you do," she threatens.

"Big deal!" says Tyler. "I could care less." He makes no move to begin the writing.

Tyler's teacher did not start off with the intention of provoking an angry power struggle with one of her students. Her goal was to stop Tyler's misbehavior and enlist his cooperation, but she was using one of the surest methods not to achieve that goal.

Discouraging messages frequently have the opposite of their intended effect. They inspire resistance, not cooperation, and lead predictably to escalating misbehavior and power struggles. Discouraging messages are the fuel for hurtful classroom dances.

Tyler's teacher doesn't realize that she set herself up for a power struggle by starting off with a signal that wasn't clear. When Tyler tests, she becomes frustrated and angry and tries to shame him into cooperation by criticizing and humiliating him in front of his peers. The focus is on Tyler's maturity, not his misbehavior. Her message conveys no confidence in his ability to cooperate or behave acceptably. In effect, she's saying: "You're not capable; I have no confidence in you; and I don't expect you to cooperate." He doesn't.

Would you feel like cooperating with someone who said these things to you? Or would you feel more inclined to retaliate? Tyler responds as many of us would—with resistance and retaliation. He perceives her message as a personal attack. He digs in his heels and launches a counterattack.

Discouraging Verbal Messages

Discouraging messages come in a variety of forms. Some are subtle and result from overinvolvement or helping too much. Others are explicit and direct such as the messages Tyler's teacher used in the previous example. All discouraging messages convey little confidence in the child's ability to make good choices and behave acceptably. They tend to personalize misbehavior and carry an underlying message of shame and blame. Let's look at the underlying message in each of the following:

Can you cooperate just once in a while?

The underlying message is "I don't believe you can cooperate." The effect is to blame, diminish, single out, and humiliate.

Show me you have a brain and make a good choice for a change!

The underlying message is "You're not very bright, and I have little confidence in your ability to make good decisions." The effect is to diminish, shame, and humiliate.

Would it be asking too much to get a little respect?

The underlying message is "I don't expect you to treat me respectfully." The effect is to blame and diminish.

Is that the best you can do?

The underlying message is "You're not very competent. You don't live up to my expectations." The effect is to shame, blame, diminish, embarrass, and humiliate.

I don't believe it! You actually did what you were asked for a change.

The underlying message is "I don't expect your cooperation." The effect is to shame, embarrass, diminish, and single out.

Try that again. I dare you.

The underlying message is "I don't expect your cooperation so continue misbehaving so I can show you I'm the boss." The effect is to challenge, provoke, blame, diminish, and intimidate.

There's one jerk in every classroom.

The underlying message is "You're not worthwhile or acceptable." The effect is to reject, shame, blame, single out, and humiliate.

Now that's real bright!

The underlying message is "You make poor decisions. I have no confidence in your ability." The effect is to diminish, shame, blame, and humiliate.

I knew I couldn't count on you.

The underlying message is "You're not capable or trustworthy. I have no confidence in your ability." The effect is to shame, blame, diminish, and humiliate.

Discouraging Action Messages

Discouraging verbal messages are overt and not difficult to recognize, but there is another type of discouraging message that is more subtle and insidious. These are action messages. Their discouraging effects are obscured by our good intentions.

Preschoolers are usually the first to point this out to us. What do they say when we offer our well-intended but unsolicited help? They usually say, "I can do it myself!"

When we do things for children that they are capable of doing for themselves, the effect can be very discouraging. The underlying message comes across something like this: "You need my help. You're not capable of doing this on your own."

Let's look at the discouraging message in each of the following examples:

A kindergartner fails on his first attempt to retie one of his shoelaces. His teacher hurries over and ties it for him.

The underlying message is "You're not capable of handling this task on your own. You need my help."

It's free activity time, and two second graders want to use the class computer. They try to work out a plan for sharing when their teacher announces, "Tina, you can use the computer first today."

The underlying message is "You're not capable of resolving this problem on your own. You need my help."

A sixth-grade teacher asks one of his students to diagram several sentences on the blackboard. The work is neat and accurate but very slow. "That's OK, Jeff," says the teacher. "I'll finish it for you."

The underlying message is "You're not doing an acceptable job. You need assistance."

Pam and Terri, two seventh graders, are chosen by their peers to organize a class party. Their teacher offers assistance. "Let's order soft drinks and pizzas and watch a video," he suggests.

The underlying message is "You're not capable of planning this party on your own. You need my help."

A thoughtful tenth grader offers to help his biology teacher clean up some laboratory equipment. "Thanks anyway, Doug," says the teacher. "This equipment is very fragile."

The underlying message is "I have little confidence in your ability to do an acceptable job."

Encouraging Messages
Inspire Cooperation

Jacob, a kindergartner, is waiting in line to go out to the playground when a classmate accidentally bumps him. Jacob gives him a push, and the boy falls down. The teacher intervenes.

"Jacob, we don't push in line," says the teacher matter-of-factly.

133

"Tommy bumped into me first," Jacob replies. "He was in my way."

"What are we supposed to do when others are in our way?" the teacher asks. Jacob just stares at her blankly.

"I don't know," he says.

"You're supposed to say 'excuse me' and wait for them to move," says the teacher.

"Sometimes they won't move," says Jacob.

"You should ask an adult for help when that happens," says the teacher. "Now you have two good choices. What are you going to do next time?"

"I'll say 'excuse me' and wait for them to move," replies Jacob. "If they don't, I'll ask you for help."

"Good!" says the teacher. "I'm sure you'll handle it fine. Now, what do you need to say to Tommy?"

"Sorry, Tommy," says Jacob.

"Thank you, Jacob," says the teacher. She gives him an appreciative smile.

Jacob's teacher used encouragement effectively. Much of her success, however, is due to the way she starts off. She begins with a limit-setting message that is both firm and respectful. No one is blamed or singled out. In a few brief sentences, she creates a positive atmosphere for problem solving. Now her encouraging words can have the greatest impact.

Where does she focus her encouragement? She focuses on better choices and actions. Then she expresses her confidence in Jacob's ability to handle the situation better next time. Her message is inspiring: "You're capable; I have confidence in you; I expect you to cooperate."

How would you feel if someone said that to you? Would you feel accepted and supported? Would you feel like cooperating? Jacob did, and so would most of us.

Encouraging messages feel good and motivate us to cooperate. They meet our needs for belonging, reaffirm our feelings of competence and self-worth, and instill confidence in our ability to handle challenging problems. Encouragement can make the difference between cooperation and resistance.

Alfred Adler, a major figure in the development of psychiatry, considered encouragement to be a fundamental component in the process of changing human behavior. His writings and those of his leading proponents continue to have a major impact on practices in education, applied psychology, and other related fields. Encouragement is gaining the recognition it deserves as an effective tool for motivating cooperative behavior. The following guidelines will help you use this tool effectively.

Guidelines for Using Encouraging Messages

Knowing what to encourage is the key to using encouragement effectively. The focus of our message should address our basic training goals. Let's review those goals briefly.

What are we trying to teach with our guidance methods? Better choices, acceptable actions, cooperation, independence, and improvement. All lead to greater responsibility. These should be the focus of our encouraging messages. Here are some examples.

Encouraging Better Choices

Often when children misbehave, they are unaware of their poor choices or that there are other, more effective, choices available. Teachers and other guidance providers are in a good position to help children explore their choices and make better ones. Consider the following.

Regina, a ninth grader, is suspended from her fourth-period class for being disruptive. She arrives at her counselor's office with a note from her teacher.

135

"What happened, Regina?" asks the counselor.

"I guess I lost my cool," Regina replies. "Sherri Mullins has been spreading rumors about me all week. I think she's jealous because we both like the same boy, but Scott has been calling me, not her. Sherri sits right behind me in my fourth-period class and whispers untrue things about Scott while we're supposed to be working. I turned around and told her to shut up. Then I called her a bitch. I guess I was kinda loud. Mrs. Swain sent me here. I'm really embarrassed."

"What do you think Sherri was trying to do?" asks her counselor.

"Make me upset," Regina replies.

"It sounds like she succeeded, too," observes her counselor. "How could you handle this differently the next time it happens?"

"I could confront her outside of class and tell her I know what she's doing," says Regina.

"Do you think she would stop if you did?" asks the counselor.

"Probably not," replies Regina upon reflection. "It would just show her that she was getting to me."

"What else could you do?" inquires the counselor.

"I could ignore her," says Regina, "but that's really hard to do, especially when she bugs me in class."

"You're right," the counselor replies. "Ignoring someone is hard to do when they sit directly behind you, but ignoring her is a good choice. She would probably stop if she saw it wasn't working. What else could you do?"

"I could ask Mrs. Swain to move me," suggests Regina.

"That's a good choice," says the counselor. "I'm sure that would help. Can you think of anything else?" Regina thought for a moment.

"Well, I guess I could ask Mrs. Swain to tell Sherri to leave me alone, but I'd prefer to leave Mrs. Swain out of it," says Regina.

"I understand," says the counselor. "You've got some good choices to use next time. I'm confident you'll handle it just fine."

Regina left her counselor's office feeling supported and encouraged. She was aware of her options, and she was prepared to make a different choice next time the situation arose.

Encouraging Acceptable Actions

Making an acceptable choice is an important first step, but getting kids to act on that choice is our larger training goal. Sometimes our encouraging words are most effective when we focus directly on actions.

For example, Cynthia, a sixth grader, knows she's not supposed to interrupt when her teacher talks to others, but Cynthia is eager to leave class for a student council meeting. She decides to interrupt anyway.

"May I go to the library, Mr. Perrin?" Cynthia asks excitedly. "My student council meeting is about to start." Mr. Perrin does not look pleased.

"Cynthia, what are you supposed to do when you want to talk to me while I'm in the middle of a conversation?" he asks.

"Wait for you to finish," replies Cynthia.

"Right," says Mr. Perrin. "Now go back to your desk and come back and try it again."

Cynthia returns to her desk, then approaches Mr. Perrin a second time. He's still talking. She waits patiently. When there's a pause in the conversation, she interjects her question. "May I go to the library for the student council meeting?"

"Sure, Cynthia," he replies, "and thank you for asking me the way you did." He gives her an appreciative smile. No feelings were hurt in this lesson. Mr. Perrin got his message across in a positive and respectful way.

Miles, a preschooler, received some instructive guidance when he used a commanding tone to get a classmate to pass some crayons.

"Give me the crayons, Jared," demands Miles. "You can't keep them all." The teacher hears him and intervenes.

"Miles, how are we supposed to ask?" Miles remembers. "Let's try it again," says his teacher.

"May I have the tray of crayons, please?" says Miles. Jared hands them over.

"Good job! Miles," says the teacher. "That's the way we like to be asked."

No shaming. No blaming. No angry words or looks of disapproval. All Miles needed was a little encouragement and an opportunity to show he could behave acceptably.

Encouraging Cooperation

We don't need misbehavior to cue us to the need for encouragement. Any time a child helps out, cooperates, or makes a contribution, we have an opportunity to use encouraging messages. Our encouragement increases the likelihood their cooperation will continue. Consider the following:

Trent, age four, notices his teacher walking toward the door with a trayful of snacks. Her hands are full. He opens the door and holds it open while she walks in.

"Thanks, Trent," says the teacher. "You're a great helper!" Trent beams with pride. The lesson wasn't lost on others.

Mr. Flores, a third-grade teacher, is called out of the classroom briefly when a parent arrives at his door. The kids have a great opportunity to clown around, but they don't. When he steps back into the room, everyone is working quietly at their seats. He appreciates their cooperation and lets them know.

"Thanks for handling things so well while I was called out," he says. "You guys are great. I knew I could count on you."

A word or two of encouragement at the right time can have a big impact. The following are just a few of the many possibilities.

"I like the way you handled that."

"Your desk looks great today."

"Good job!"

"Your helping out makes a big difference."

"I knew I could count on you."

"Thanks, I appreciate your thoughtfulness."

Encouraging Independence

One of our larger guidance goals is to assist children to handle problems on their own. We do this by teaching effective problem-solving skills and by limiting our involvement so children have opportunities to practice those skills independently. Encouragement plays an important role in the process. It gives children the confidence to take risks and act independently. Consider the following:

Evan, a fifth grader, runs to tattle on a classmate. "Mr. Kilmer, Damen was copying from my paper."

"Did you ask him to stop or cover up your paper so he couldn't?" asks Mr. Kilmer.

"Well, no," replies Evan, expecting the teacher to handle it.

"Then that's what you need to do if it happens again," says Mr. Kilmer, with a smile. "I'm sure you'll handle it fine."

Nick and Carla, two kindergartners, quarrel over a scooter. "Give it to me," screams Carla, loud enough to attract her teacher's attention. It works. As the teacher approaches, both kids clutch the scooter tightly. "I think you guys can work this out," says the teacher confidently. "Do you remember our plan for sharing?" Nick does. He runs back into the classroom and returns a few moments later with a timer. He sets it for five minutes. "I get to use it first," he announces.

"OK," says Carla reluctantly, "but I get to use it next." "You sure do," says the teacher. "Good job, guys! You handled it just fine. I knew you could."

Mrs. Ehlers, a seventh-grade science teacher, passes out an assignment to the class. Less than a minute goes by before Barry comes up for his own personal set of instructions. "I don't understand what I'm supposed to do," he says.

"Did you read the directions carefully and think about what you're supposed to do?" the teacher asks.

"I think so," Barry replies, hoping she will do the thinking for him.

"Well, try it again," says his teacher in an encouraging voice. "I'm confident you can figure it out on your own. If you still aren't sure after five minutes, I'll be happy to help."

"Rats!" Barry says to himself. "She didn't go for it." He heads back to his seat to figure it out on his own.

Five minutes later, Barry is busy with his assignment. He may not realize it, but he just received a lesson in independence. His teacher's encouragement and reluctance to rescue him made it possible.

Encouraging Improvement

Some skills, such as taking turns or learning not to interrupt, require repeated effort and practice before they can be mastered. The process is gradual. Adult impatience or expectations of immediate mastery can be very discouraging. Our energy is best directed toward encouraging improvement. The focus should be on effort, not outcome; process not product.

Brad, a third grader, lives in a home where interrupting is OK. Whenever he has something to say, he just says it. His parents usually stop whatever they're doing and give him their undivided attention.

At school, things are different. Interrupting is not OK. When Brad interrupts, his teacher asks him to raise his hand and wait to be called. They've been practicing this skill for months, but progress has been slow. Brad's teacher feels frustrated.

"Maybe I should make him sit at the back table for five minutes each time he interrupts," Brad's teacher suggests to a colleague. "Maybe that will help him remember." The colleague has another suggestion.

"Try using encouragement first and see what happens," she suggests. "Each time he remembers to raise his hand, let him know how much you appreciate it. When he needs prompts, thank him after he does it the right way."

The next morning, Brad wants to ask a question and remembers to raise his hand without prompts. "Thank you, Brad," says his teacher. "I really appreciate it when you raise your hand." He looks pleased.

Later in the day, Brad starts to blurt out an answer without being called on. "What are you supposed to do when you want to be called on, Brad?" asks his teacher. Brad remembers and raises his hand. "Thank you, Brad," she says with an appreciative smile. His teacher decides to continue the plan for a full month.

Several weeks later, the same colleague inquires about Brad's progress. "How's he doing?" she asks.

"Much better," replies Brad's teacher. "He remembers more than he forgets. In fact, he hasn't interrupted for several days." Encouragement is making a difference.

Involving Parents in the Encouragement Process

One of the best ways to increase the motivational power of encouragement is to involve parents in the process. When parents and teachers combine their encouraging efforts, children feel even more inspired to make good choices and cooperate.

At the preschool and elementary levels, it's an effective practice to send home special commendations, awards, or certificates of merit acknowledging student effort, cooperation, or achievement. The commendations can be included with other materials in the student's Friday folder. At the secondary level, a personal note to the parents or a phone call has the same effect.

The gesture is rewarding for everybody. Parents like to hear the good news and enjoy sharing that news with their child. The child feels good about having his or her efforts publicly acknowledged. Teachers gain a lot of cooperation and respect from parents and students by simply acknowledging what has taken place. The small investment yields big returns in cooperation.

Chapter Summary

In this chapter, we examined two contrasting approaches to motivating children. We saw how discouraging messages, which often accompany soft limits, achieve the opposite of their intended effect. They inspire resistance, not cooperation, and fuel power struggles and classroom dances.

Encouraging messages, on the other hand, are highly effective motivational tools, particularly when used with firm limits. Encouraging messages meet children's needs for belonging, reaffirm feelings of competence and self-worth, and inspire children to tackle challenging tasks and problems on their own. Encouraging messages can make the difference between cooperation and resistance (Figure 7A).

Knowing what to encourage is the key to using encouragement effectively. Our messages have their greatest impact when they focus on better choices, acceptable actions, cooperation, independence, and improvement.

Figure 7A. Encouraging vs. discouraging messages

Encouraging messages	Discouraging messages
Inspire cooperation	Inspire resistance, retaliation
Motivate and empower	Discourage and humiliate
Convey respect, confidence, support	Diminish, blame, reject
	Create adversarial relationships
Create cooperative relationships	Perceived as personal attack
Meet needs for belonging, competence, self-worth	Focus on child's worth and capabilities
Focus on choices and behavior	

Chapter

8

Teaching Problem-Solving Skills

If you didn't know how to play tennis and I lectured you for two hours about playing a match, would that make you a competent tennis player? Not likely. You would have to get out on the tennis court and practice your skills many times before that would happen, and you would probably need more instruction.

Children learn problem-solving skills in much the same way. Our words help the process along, but information alone is sometimes not enough. They may need practice and additional instruction before they can fully master the skills we're trying to teach.

In this chapter, you'll learn four simple and effective strategies for teaching children problem-solving skills. Your consistent application of these techniques will provide your students with the instruction and practice they need to become better problem solvers.

Providing Information Is Sometimes Not Enough

I like to tell the story about Kaley and her lunch box because it illustrates a principle about how children learn that is so fundamental it is often overlooked. Kaley, age six, and her mother arrived at my office with an interesting dilemma. Each day Kaley left for school with a carefully prepared lunch, but the best items in her lunch box always seemed to end up in some other child's hands. Often Kaley arrived home in tears.

"I don't understand it," said her frustrated mother. "She knows what to do. I've told her over and over again to say no when older kids ask for her lunch items. Her teacher and principal have done the same thing, but Kaley continues to give them away! Her teacher says there's nothing she can do if Kaley chooses to give her lunch away."

Kaley probably did know what to do, but I wanted to check this out myself to be sure.

"Kaley, what are you supposed to do when other kids ask for your lunch items?" I asked. She parroted back the words her mother, teacher, and principal told her.

"I'm supposed to say no and tell the teacher if they take them anyway," she said.

Her mother was right. On an intellectual level, Kaley understood what she was supposed to do. But knowing what to do and actually doing it are two different things. I suspected her skill training was incomplete, so I explored the problem a little further.

"Saying no to big kids is sometimes hard to do," I said. Kaley nodded her agreement.

"I get scared," she said.

"Let's practice saying no to big kids for a while," I suggested. "Maybe we can help you feel more comfortable." I wanted Kaley to see, hear, and feel what it is like to do what she was being asked.

I pretended that a book was her lunch box, and I asked Kaley's mother to be the big kid while I pretended to be Kaley. When her mother made a pitch for my chips, I said, "No, they're mine. You can't have them." We went through this procedure several times, and each time I role-modeled different ways to say no. I said no in a loud voice and a soft voice, with eye contact and without eye contact, but each time, I held on tightly to the lunch box and waited until her mother walked away.

"Now it's your turn to practice, Kaley," I said. "This time, I'll pretend to be the big kid, and you can hold the lunch box." I approached her and asked for the chips. She didn't make eye contact, but she did say no very clearly.

"That was a clear no," I said. "That will work just fine. Let's try it again."

We repeated the scenario many times. Each time, I encouraged her to say no a different way to see which way felt most comfortable. She preferred the simple two-word approach, "No, sorry," and she discovered that she felt more comfortable when she didn't have to look at me while she said it. She was gaining confidence.

"Ready to try this at school?" I asked.

"I guess so," Kaley replied.

I asked her mother to practice the procedure with Kaley a few more times before she left for school the next day. We scheduled a follow-up appointment for later that week.

"How did it go?" I asked when they arrived for the follow-up visit. I could tell from the look on Kaley's face that she had enjoyed some success.

"It went fine," said her mother. "The practice really helped. Her lunch stayed in her hands all week." Kaley had a proud look of accomplishment.

"Congratulations!" I said. She was well on her way to mastering an important skill.

What made the difference? Kaley needed practice and further instruction before she could master the skill her mother and others were trying to teach. The information they provided was a helpful first step, but it didn't go far enough. Kaley knew what to do but not how to do it. Her skill training was incomplete. The simple technique of role-modeling plus a little encouragement helped her complete the lesson others had begun.

Many children find themselves in situations like Kaley's where they know what to do but not how to do it. They need more than information. Simply telling them to walk away from a fight, ignore someone who teases, or just say no when peers encourage them to experiment with drugs or alcohol may not be enough. They may need further instruction and opportunities to practice before they can master the skill we're trying to teach. Let's look at several guidance strategies that provide students with the instruction and practice they need to complete the skill-training sequence.

Role-Modeling Corrective Behavior

Role-modeling corrective behavior is a simple and effective guidance strategy with varied applications. It can be used to teach independent problem-solving skills as in the example of Kaley or to teach corrective behavior when students misbehave because they lack the skills to behave differently.

The procedure is concrete and therefore particularly effective with younger children, from ages two to seven. It provides them with opportunities to see, hear, feel, and practice the corrective action we want them to carry out. When misbehavior is not involved in the lesson, use the following steps:

1. Role-model the corrective behavior you want the child to use.

2. Encourage the child to try it again using the corrective behavior. Practice several times, if needed.

3. Encourage effort and improvement.

For example, Miss Casey, a preschool teacher, wants her students to get ready to go outside. "It's time to pick up whatever you're using and put it away," she announces. "We need to get ready for recess."

Hilda, age three, hears her teacher and hurriedly throws most of the blocks she's using into their container. Then she places the container on the shelf. "I'm ready," she says.

"Are you sure you're ready, Hilda?" asks Miss Casey, noticing several blocks are still scattered on the floor and that Hilda's carpet strip hasn't been put away.

Hilda nods, convinced.

"Well, you're close," says Miss Casey. "Let me show you what your area should look like when you're ready." She places a carpet strip down on the floor and pours out a container of blocks next to the carpet strip. While Hilda watches, Miss Casey picks up all the blocks, puts them in the container, and returns the container to the shelf. Then she puts away the carpet strip.

"Does your area look like this?" asks Miss Casey. Hilda shakes her head. "Then you need to finish the job. I'm sure you'll do fine." Hilda does.

Now let's look at another application of this technique. When teaching corrective behavior following an incident of misbehavior, use the following steps:

1. Provide a clear, firm-limit-setting message.

2. Role-model the acceptable corrective behavior.

3. Encourage the child to try it again using the corrective behavior.

4. Encourage effort and improvement.

For example, Joel, a fourth grader, becomes frustrated when the student who sits behind him taps the back of Joel's chair. Joel can't concentrate on his work.

"Cut it out, butthead!" shouts Joel angrily. His teacher intervenes.

"Joel, we don't talk like that in the classroom," says the teacher matter-of-factly. "Do you need some quiet time to cool down?" He shakes his head.

"Chris was tapping the back of my chair, and he has been bugging me all morning," complains Joel. "I'm sick of it!"

"What are you supposed to do when other kids bother or tease you?" asks the teacher. Joel looks at him blankly.

"I don't know," he replies.

"Well, you could ask him politely to stop or ask me to help if he doesn't," says the teacher. "Watch how I do it." He turns to Chris and says, "Chris, please stop tapping my desk." He pauses briefly to let his words sink in, then looks at Chris.

"Would that work, Chris?" he asks. Chris nods.

"Good!" says the teacher. "That's all there is to it. Now you try it, Joel. Tell Chris what he needs to know." Joel turns to Chris and practices the skill.

"Thanks, guys," says the teacher. "That works much better."

In another classroom, Mr. Simmons, uses role modeling to deal with a disrespectful tenth grader. Mr. Simmons is a popular teacher. He runs an informal class and believes the relaxed atmosphere helps his students feel comfortable. He's probably right, but some students misinterpret his good intentions and push things too far. Brad is a good example.

"Hey, Simmons," says Brad in a disrespectful tone. "Give me the hall pass. I need to use the restroom." Mr. Simmons calls Brad up to his desk.

"I'd be happy to give you a hall pass, Brad," says Mr. Simmons matter-of-factly, "but not when you ask me like that. Can you think of another way to ask?" Brad looks at him impatiently and rolls his eyes.

"Come on. Just give it to me," says Brad with the same impatient tone. He expects Mr. Simmons to become rattled and give in, but Mr. Simmons keeps his cool and remains firm.

"Maybe it would help if I showed you how to ask," Mr. Simmons suggests. "Try this: 'May I use the hall pass for a trip to the restroom?' That will always work."

"OK. Have it your way," says Brad, realizing Mr. Simmon's resolve. "May I use the hall pass to go to the bathroom?"

"Sure," replies Mr. Simmons with an appreciative smile. "Thanks for asking the way you did."

Yes, role-modeling corrective behavior even works with teens, but it's not easy to keep our composure when students are as disrespectful as Brad. Mr. Simmons was very effective. He taught the skill he wanted Brad to learn and role-modeled the respect he wanted Brad to show. No one was blamed or singled out. The lesson was a win-win situation for both of them.

Try It Again

Try it again is a simple, concrete, and highly effective guidance procedure that is used almost intuitively by preschool teachers to address minor misbehaviors. The applications of this procedure, however, extend well beyond the preschool level. It can be used with older children and teens as well.

The procedure is easy to carry out. After an incident of minor misbehavior, state a firm limit-setting message and encourage the child to carry out the corrective behavior with the words, "Try it again." The focus is on corrective action, not the offending behavior. The child is simply given another opportunity to demonstrate that he or she can make a better choice and cooperate. If the child chooses instead to resist, then this procedure leads smoothly to limited choices or logical consequences. Consider the following examples.

A group of preschoolers run into the classroom yelling and creating a disturbance. Their teacher intervenes.

"Guys, we're supposed to use indoor voices in the classroom." She leads them outside. "Let's try it again the right way." They do.

Marla, a fifth grader, is working on a writing assignment when her pen runs out of ink. She asks the teacher to lend her another, but all of his pens are blue. She needs a black pen.

"Will someone lend Marla a black pen?" he asks.

"I will," says Dave. He pulls out a black pen and flings it across the room for Marla to catch. He can tell, by the look on his teacher's face, that the aerial display wasn't appreciated.

"Dave, how are we supposed to pass things in the classroom?" asks the teacher.

"We're supposed to hand them to each other," Dave replies.

"Right," says the teacher. "Please pick up the pen and try it again." Dave picks the pen up off the floor then walks over to Marla and hands it to her.

"Thanks, Dave," says the teacher. "I appreciate your helping out."

Abby, a ninth grader, is unhappy because she has to go to the attendance office to pick up a tardy slip. When the teacher hands Abby a hall pass, Abby snatches it from her teacher's hand.

"Let's try that again," says her teacher matter-of-factly. She holds out the hall pass for Abby to take once again and waits patiently for her to take it the right way. Abby does.

"Thanks, Abby," says the teacher.

Abby's teacher is effective. She keeps her cool and role-models the respect and cooperation she expects.

Providing Limited Choices

Danny, age nine, is a great kickball player, but his sportsmanship needs improvement. Sometimes when his turn is over, he refuses to go to the sidelines and tries to persuade others to let him have another turn. When the yard-duty teacher sees what he's doing, she intervenes.

"Danny, you can play by the rules and go to the sidelines when you're out, or you'll have to find another game to play today. What would you like to do?"

"OK," says Danny. Reluctantly, he goes to the back of the line.

"Thanks for cooperating," says the teacher.

The yard-duty teacher is using limited choices, a highly effective method for teaching decision making and responsibility. The way she sets up this situation, Danny cannot avoid being responsible for his behavior. His options are clear, and so are the consequences associated with each choice. In this case, he chooses to cooperate.

Let's say, for the sake of argument, that Danny makes a different choice. He decides to test and continues to resist following the rules. What should the teacher do? She should follow through with a logical consequence and remove his kickball privileges for the remainder of the day. Either way, Danny learns the intended lesson. Both choices, acceptable or unacceptable, lead to effective learning.

Guidelines for Using Limited Choices

1. Remember, these are limited choices, with an emphasis on the word *limited*. Restrict the number of choices you present to two or three and be sure the desired

153

corrective step is one of them. For example, if you don't want your students to play with baseball cards during class, you might say: "Guys, you can play with baseball cards during recess, lunch, or after school, but not during class. If you have them out during class again, I'll have to take them away and keep them in my desk until the next teacher-parent conference." Now, the kids have all the information they need to make an acceptable choice. All you need to do is follow through.

2. The choices you present represent your limits. State them firmly with no wiggle room, or you may invite testing. For example, if you don't want your students to wear hats in class, you might say: "You can wear hats in the hallway or on the playground, but not in the classroom. If you wear them in the classroom again, I'll have to put them in my hat drawer. You can have them back after school on Fridays." This message is clear and firm.

   Choices presented with soft limits reduce the effectiveness of this guidance procedure. For example, imagine a teacher in the above example saying: "I'd prefer that you wear your hats on the playground or in the hallways, OK?" This message lacks firmness. The teacher can expect testing from aggressive researchers.

3. After you present the choices, ask the question: "What would you like to do?" The question places the responsibility for decision making and corrective action where it belongs—on the child's shoulders. In effect, you're saying: "You control your choices. What choice would you like to make?"

4. When students say they will cooperate but fail to do so, follow through with a logical consequence (action message) that supports your rules. Don't be seduced into giving reminders, repeating the choices, or trying further persuasion. The time for talking has passed. It's time for action. Follow through.

Questions About Limited Choices

1. *What should I do when I present the choices but the child introduces new choices or attempts to engage me in bargaining?*

Answer: Some children, particularly those trained with permissiveness, are skillful at changing limited choices into "Let's make a deal." This is limit testing. When children attempt to introduce additional choices, say, "That's not one of your choices."

When children attempt to engage you in bargaining or arguments, you should say firmly, "Those are your only choices. What would you like to do?" Use the cut-off technique if needed.

2. *Should I use limited choices with children who frequently test or violate my rules?*

Answer: Yes. Limited choices are effective with aggressive researchers, too, but you'll need to specify a logical consequence for noncompliance at the same time you present the choices. For example, if you ask one of your students to stop shoving in line, and you expect testing, you might say, "James, you can keep your hands to yourself or you can wait in the back of the line next to me. What would you like to do?"

Now James has all the information he needs to make an acceptable choice. If he wants to keep his place in line, he'll cooperate. If he chooses instead to test or violate your rule, follow through with your logical consequence and ask him to go to the back of the line. Either way, James will learn that he is responsible for his choices.

3. *What should I do when I present the limited choices, but the child refuses to answer or responds with a blank stare?*

Answer: If you suspect the child has tuned out, use the check-in procedure. If you suspect the child is intentionally ignoring you, then let him or her know that no response is the same as a refusal. Follow through with a logical consequence. The child will soon discover that a decision not to choose is also a choice.

Examples of Limited Choices

The following examples illustrate some of the many ways limited choices can be used. Often this guidance procedure leads to an acceptable choice, but I've also included examples where children respond with testing or defiance so you can see how to follow up with an instructive logical consequence.

It's lunchtime, and Harry, a preschooler, tries to amuse his friends by taking bites of his peanut-butter-and-jelly sandwich, then opening his mouth to reveal the contents. His teacher asks him to stop, and he does for a while, then starts again. His teacher gives him some choices.

"Harry, you can sit with the group if you eat your lunch the right way. You'll have to sit by yourself and eat at the back table if you don't. What would you like to do?" she asks. Eating alone is no fun. Harry decides to cooperate.

Jessica, a third grader, is a talented jump roper, but she isn't very tolerant of others with less skill. Sometimes when others attempt difficult tricks, Jessica swings the rope extra fast to end their turn. When the yard-duty teacher sees what Jessica is doing, she intervenes.

"Jessica, you can play the right way or find another game to play," says the teacher. "What would you like to do?"

"I'll play the right way," says Jessica, but a few minutes later, she's back to her old tricks. This time the teacher follows through with the logical consequence.

"You'll have to find another game to play for today, Jessica," says the teacher matter-of-factly. "You can try jump rope again tomorrow." Jessica will probably think carefully next time she decides to end someone's turn.

It's recess, and a group of boys play catch with a Frisbee on the blacktop. Frisbees are allowed only on the playfields. The yard-duty teacher gives them some choices. "You guys can play Frisbee in the south field or the north field. What would you like to do?" she asks.

"Can we throw it from the play structure?" asks one student.

"No. That isn't one of your choices," says the teacher. They head off to play in the south field.

Maria, a sixth grader, refuses to go to the time-out area after being disruptive. Her teacher gives her some choices.

"Maria, you can spend ten quiet minutes at the back table or twenty quiet minutes in Mr. Dicksen's class next door. What would you like to do?"

"Ten is better than twenty," Maria thinks to herself. Reluctantly, she heads to the back table.

It's the third week of school, and Manny, a seventh grader, continues to disrupt his science class every day. His teacher has used time-outs consistently, but the pattern continues. She suspects she may need assistance from Manny's parents. After class, she presents the option to Manny with limited choices.

"Manny, I've tried to help you stop disrupting class for three weeks, but we haven't made much progress. Can we work this out between the two of us, or do we need some help from your parents?" Manny is sure he wants to keep his parents out of it.

"I think we can work it out," he replies.

"I hope so," says the teacher, "but if we can't, I'll have to schedule a conference with your parents." Now, the consequence for continued disruption is clear. All the teacher needs to do is follow through.

Bev and Sandy, both seniors, sit next to each other in their second-period class. They're good students, but they also like to talk. Their talking has become a problem. The teacher gives them some choices.

"Bev and Sandy, you can sit together without talking, or you'll have to sit apart. What would you like to do?"

"We'd like to sit together," says Sandy. Bev nods in agreement. They made their choices. Now, all the teacher needs to do is follow through.

Sid, a tenth grader, knows it's not OK to wear a bandanna in class but does it anyway. When his teacher asks him to take it off, he refuses. She gives him some choices.

"You can put the bandanna away or you can work it out with Mr. Clayborn, our vice principal," she says matter-of-factly. "What would you like to do?" Sid knows what will happen if he has to deal with Mr. Clayborn. Reluctantly, he removes the bandanna.

Exploring Choices

Sometimes, children are unaware of other, more effective, choices for solving problems. Exploring choices is an instructive guidance procedure that helps children consider alternative choices for behavior. The procedure can be used as a training step after consequences have been applied or to teach problem solving when no misbehavior has occurred.

From a developmental perspective, exploring choices is most appropriate for older children and teens because it requires abstract-thinking skills. You can adapt the procedure for younger children as well, but you will probably need to suggest the choices yourself and combine the procedure with try it again and role modeling to make the experience more concrete.

When a child makes a poor choice or is unsure about how to solve a problem, use the following steps:

1. In a question format, explore with the child other available choices for solving the problem.
2. Encourage the child to select and carry out one of the better choices.

For example, five-year-old Shawn completes a five-minute time-out for pushing another child. When the time-out is over, his teacher helps him explore other, more effective, choices for handling the situation.

"Shawn, pushing Robert when he teased you was not a good choice. Pushing others will always result in a time-out. What can you do the next time Robert teases you?" she asks.

"I don't know," Shawn replies.

"You could politely ask him not to with your words," suggests the teacher. She role-models how to do it. "Or, you could walk away and try to ignore him. If he continues, you could ask me for help. What are you going to do next time?"

"I'll ask him to stop," says Shawn, "and I'll try to ignore him if he doesn't."

"Good plan!" says his teacher. "That should work, and if it doesn't, I'll be happy to help."

Paula, a sixth grader, is upset because she received partial credit on a late assignment. She appeals her case to her teacher.

"It's not fair!" complains Paula. "I finished the assignment on time. I just forgot to bring it in."

"That is frustrating," acknowledges her teacher. "What can you do to prevent this from happening again?"

"I could ask my mom to remind me," says Paula.

"That's one choice, but whose job is it to keep track of your assignments?" asks the teacher.

"It's mine," Paula replies. "She probably wouldn't do it, anyway."

"What else could you do?" inquires her teacher. "I notice you never forget to bring your backpack. Is that part of the solution?"

"That's a great idea!" says Paula. "I leave my backpack in the front entry when I get home. I'll take it to my room and put my homework inside it when it's done. Then I'll never forget it."

"You solved that problem!" says the teacher.

Blake, a high-school senior, arrives at his counselor's office upset. "I can't stand Mr. Crocker," Blake complains. "He should have become a drill sergeant instead of a teacher. He loves to order people around and make them feel stupid. I want to drop his class."

"It's not too late to drop the class," says the counselor, "but are you sure that's what you want to do?"

"I'm sure!" says Blake emphatically. He sounds determined, but his counselor isn't sure that dropping the class is the best alternative. He helps Blake explore his choices.

"You need two semesters of a foreign language to graduate," says the counselor, "and this is your last semester. It's too late to enroll in another Spanish class. If you drop Mr. Crocker's class, how will you fulfill your language requirement before graduation?"

"I hadn't thought of that," confesses Blake. "If I take Spanish during summer school, could I still graduate with my class?"

"I think so," replies the counselor, "but is that what you really want to do? You have a solid B in Mr. Crocker's class now and six weeks left in the semester. Are you ready to spend four weeks of your summer repeating work you've already completed?"

"Not exactly," says Blake. "My dad expects me to get a job. He would be pretty angry with me if I had to take summer school." Blake's dilemma was coming into perspective. "Maybe sticking it out in Mr. Crocker's class is worth considering," suggests the counselor. "What can you do to make it more bearable?"

"I guess I'll just have to bite my lip when he tries to humiliate me or order me around," says Blake.

"You have my support if you need someone to talk to," says the counselor.

Blake received a valuable lesson in problem solving. By the time they were done, he understood his choices and the consequences associated with each. No one needed to tell him what to do. The technique of exploring choices helped him arrive at the best solution on his own.

Chapter Summary

Providing information is an important first step when teaching children problem-solving skills, but information alone may not be enough. Sometimes children need practice and additional instruction before they can master the skills we're trying to teach. In this chapter, we examined four methods that provide both the information and instructive experiences children need to become better problem solvers. Role modeling, try it again, limited choices, and exploring choices will help your students master the lessons you're trying to teach and become better problem solvers in the process.

How to Use Consequences to Support Your Rules

So far, you've learned how to give clear signals with your words, how to inspire cooperation with encouragement, and how to teach problem solving when children lack the skills to do what you request. These steps provide all the verbal information children need to behave acceptably, but as you know, your words are only the first part of your total message.

Children may still decide to test, and when they do, the time for talking is over. It's time to act. You must answer their research questions with concrete action messages that they really understand. Consequences are the second part of your limit-setting message. They speak louder than words.

This chapter will show you how to use consequences to stop misbehavior and teach your rules in the clearest and most understandable way. If you've relied on permissiveness in the past, you'll discover how to use consequences to regain your credibility and authority and to teach your students to tune back in to your words. If you've relied on punishment in the past, you'll discover how to build cooperative relationships with your students based on mutual respect rather than fear and intimidation. For anyone recovering from a bad case of soft limits, the consequences in this chapter will be a big step in the direction of effective communication and problem solving.

Why Consequences Are Important

Consequences are like walls. They stop misbehavior. They provide clear and definitive answers to children's research questions about what's acceptable and who's in charge, and they teach responsibility by holding children accountable for their choices and behavior. When used consistently, consequences define the path you want your students to stay on and teach them to tune in to your words.

If you've relied on permissive or punitive methods in the past, you will probably need to use consequences often during the first four to eight weeks that you implement the guidance strategies in this book. Why? Because your aggressive researchers will probably test you frequently to determine if things are really different. This is the only way they will know that your rules have changed and that your walls are really solid. You are likely to hear comments such as "You're not fair!" or "You're mean!" as they attempt to break down your walls and get you to revert back to your old behavior.

This is what Mr. Harvey discovered when he attended one of my workshops looking for more effective ways to handle the daily testing, resistance, and arguments he was encountering in the classroom. It didn't take him long to recognize that his permissive approach was part of the problem. His limits were soft, and his consequences, if he used them at all, were late and ineffective. His kids were taking advantage of him, and he was eager to put an end to it. After he completed my workshop, he made an announcement to his class.

"I'll be running the classroom differently from now on," Mr. Harvey began. "I'm not going to repeat my directions anymore or remind you to do the things you're supposed to do. I'm not going to argue or debate if you don't want to do it. I will only ask you once. If you decide not to cooperate, then I will use consequences to hold you accountable." He explained logical consequences and the time-out procedure.

"He doesn't mean it," whispered one student. "Yeah, he knows who's really in charge here," chuckled another. Their reaction was understandable. Their previous experiences gave them little cause to regard his words seriously.

But Mr. Harvey kept his word. When he gave directions or requested their cooperation, he said it only once. No more repeating or reminding. When the kids ignored him or tuned out, he used the check-in procedure. When they tried to argue or debate, he used the cut-off technique. If they persisted, he followed through quickly with logical consequences or time-out.

"What got into him?" wondered several students at the end of the first week. "Yeah, we liked him better the old way."

The methods worked. For the first time, Mr. Harvey's students were accountable for their poor choices and behavior. They were learning to be responsible, but their testing didn't let up for a while.

In fact, their testing intensified during the first few weeks. His aggressive researchers did everything they could to wear him down and get him to revert back to his old ways. It didn't work. He didn't give in or compromise, even when they told him he was mean or unfair. He was prepared for their resistance.

An initial increase in testing during the first four weeks is a normal and expected part of the learning and change process. After all, Mr. Harvey told his students things were going to be different. How could they know for sure that he really meant what he said? Of course, they had to test and see for themselves. When they did, Mr. Harvey answered their questions with instructive consequences.

Four weeks after he started, Mr. Harvey noticed a change. The change was subtle at first, not dramatic. There was less testing and more cooperation. The kids were tuning back in to his words. They were beginning to change their beliefs about his rules.

Your consequences will accomplish your immediate goal of stopping your students' misbehavior when it occurs, but teaching them to tune back in to your words will take time. How much time? This depends on your consistency, the length of time you've been using soft limits, and the amount of training your students need to be convinced that your rules have changed.

As you accumulate hours of consistency between your words and actions, you will notice less testing and less need for consequences. This will be your signal that your students are tuning back in. They are beginning to change their beliefs about your rules.

What Makes a Consequence Effective?

The effectiveness of your consequences depends largely on how you apply them. If you apply them in a punitive or permissive manner, your consequences will have limited training value. You'll be teaching different lessons than you intend, and you, not your students, will be responsible for most of the problem solving. If you apply consequences in a democratic manner, however, your signals will be clear, and so will the lessons you're trying to teach. Consequences are most effective when used democratically.

Let me illustrate this point by showing how three teachers can use the same consequence for the same misbehavior with varying degrees of effectiveness. Mr. Wallace uses the permissive approach. When he sees Kenny cheating at tetherball, he gives Kenny a lecture on the importance of honesty and fair play and asks him to sit out his next turn. "What a joke!" Kenny says to himself. Within minutes, he's back to his old tricks.

Mrs. Hunter uses the punitive approach. When she sees Kenny cheating at tetherball, she singles him out for humiliation. "Nobody likes to play with a cheater!" she says in a loud, accusatory voice. "If you can't play fair, you won't play at all. No more tetherball for a week."

"A week!" exclaims Kenny. "That's not fair!" He walks off feeling resentful and considers ways to get back.

Miss Fisher uses the democratic approach. When she sees Kenny cheating, she calls him aside respectfully. "Kenny, you can't play tetherball if you don't play by the rules," she says matter-of-factly. "You need to find another game to play for the rest of this recess. You can try tetherball again next recess." No lectures. No humiliation. No long or drawn-out consequences. Next recess, Kenny plays by the rules.

Each of the teachers in these examples decided to limit Kenny's tetherball time as a consequence for not playing by the rules. Mr. Wallace applied the consequence permissively. His message was respectful, but his consequence lacked firmness. It was too brief. Kenny continued testing.

Mrs. Hunter applied the consequence punitively. Her message was more than firm. It was harsh and not very respectful. Kenny understood the rule she was trying to teach, but he didn't feel good about the way her message was delivered. He left their encounter feeling resentful with no greater desire to cooperate.

Miss Fisher applied the consequence in a democratic manner. Her message was both firm and respectful. Her consequence achieved the right balance between the two extremes. It wasn't too long, and it wasn't too brief. It was instructive. No feelings were injured. No relationships were damaged. Kenny received the information he needed to make a better choice. He didn't need a week to show that he could cooperate.

Miss Fisher was effective because she understands how to use consequences. Let's look at the properties effective consequences share in common.

Immediacy

It's snack time, and Ricky, age four, decides to blow bubbles in his carton of milk. His classmates are amused, but not his teacher. She gives him some choices. "Ricky, it's not OK to blow bubbles in your milk. You can drink it the right way, or you'll have to put it away. What would you like to do?"

"I'll drink it the right way," says Ricky. He does, too, for a while, but as soon as his teacher leaves, he decides to test. He puts the carton to his lips and blows some more big bubbles. Without any further words, his teacher removes the milk carton. Ricky will have another chance to drink the right way next time they have snacks.

Consequences are most effective when they are applied immediately after the unacceptable behavior. The immediacy of the consequence helped Ricky make the cause-and-effect connection between his misbehavior and the consequence he experienced. The lesson was instructive. If his teacher had chosen instead to overlook his misbehavior and withhold his milk during the next snack period, her consequence would have had much less impact.

Consistency

Tina, an eighth grader, loves to visit with friends between classes, but her next class is PE, and she doesn't want to be late. Last time she arrived late to PE, she had to go to the office for a tardy slip and lost points for missing calisthenics.

"I'll be careful," Tina says to herself. She keeps an eye on her watch and continues to visit. With one minute to go, she sprints for class and nearly makes it. Her teacher greets her at the door.

"Hi, Tina," says Mrs. Perles, as she points in the direction of the attendance office. "I'll see you after you pick up a tardy slip."

"Not again!" says Tina remorsefully. She searches for a good excuse. "I had trouble with my locker," she says convincingly. "Can't this be an exception, please?"

Mrs. Perles holds firm. "Sorry, Tina," she says. "You can explain your situation to Mr. Harris, our vice principal, if you wish, but there's nothing more I can do."

Tina is determined to avoid consequences if she can. When she appeals her case to Mr. Harris, he also holds firm. "Ten minutes is plenty of time to get to class," he says. "I'm sure you'll be more careful next time."

"Rats!" Tina says to herself. "He's as tight as Mrs. Perles." She picks up her tardy slip and heads back to class.

Consistent consequences are vital to effective guidance. Your consistency helps children collect the data they need to arrive at the conclusions you intend. Some students, like Tina, need to collect a lot of data before they are convinced, but the process is the same for all. Tina will learn that she is expected and required to show up for class on time.

As the example illustrates, consistency has many dimensions. There's consistency between our words and our actions. There's consistency between the classroom and the office, and there's consistency between the way consequences are applied from one time to the next. Tina experienced consistency in all of these areas. She received the clearest possible signal about her school's rule.

Let's say, for the sake of argument, that Tina's PE teacher is only 60 percent consistent about enforcing her rule about showing up for class on time. What can she expect from Tina and others? More testing? Of course. In reality, the rule is only in effect 60 percent of the time. How will the kids know when it is and is not in effect? They will have to test. Inconsistency is an invitation for testing.

Relatedness

When we fail to pay our phone bills for several months, does the phone company respond by disconnecting our cable TV service? No. That would not stop us from using our phone without paying. Instead, they use a consequence that is logically related to the behavior they want to change. They shut off our phone service and charge us a reinstallation fee when they hook us back up. This teaches us to be more responsible about paying for our phone service.

Children also learn best when the consequences they experience are logically related to their behavior. It makes little sense to take away a child's recess privileges or an upcoming field trip because that child decides to bother a classmate during instruction. What does annoying others have to do with recesses or field trips? The consequences and the offending behavior are not logically related.

A more instructive consequence would be to temporarily separate the student from others and provide him with some time to get back under control. The message might sound like: "Jimmy, you need to move your desk about five feet away from Ben. You can move back to your old spot after lunch." Jimmy hears stop and experiences stopping. The consequence is both immediate and logically related to the behavior we want to change. Jimmy has the data he needs to make a better choice.

Duration

Stephanie, a second grader, makes disruptive noises while her classmates work quietly at their seats. The teacher tries to ignore the noise, but it gets louder. Finally, she walks over and asks Stephanie to stop. Stephanie does, for a while, then starts up again a few minutes later.

"I've had enough of your rudeness!" says the teacher angrily. She sends Stephanie to the office and tells her not to return until after lunch. It's only nine-thirty.

Sure, the consequence stopped Stephanie's disruptive behavior, but it also eliminated all her opportunities to demonstrate that she could cooperate and behave acceptably during the remainder of the morning. A brief five- or ten-minute time-out would have accomplished the teacher's purpose adequately.

When it comes to applying consequences, more is not necessarily better. Consequences of brief duration often achieve our training goals more effectively than long-term consequences, particularly with preschool and elementary-school children. Why? Because brief consequences, applied consistently, give children more opportunities to collect data and make acceptable choices. More teaching and learning occur.

This principle is difficult for many teachers who operate from the punitive model to accept. From their perspective, if a little is good, then a lot must be wonderful. They tend to go overboard with the length or severity of their consequences, then they add to their own frustration by expecting change to happen rapidly. They don't realize that long, drawn-out consequences actually slow down the training process by providing fewer opportunities for learning. Worse yet, teachers must endure the resentment their consequences cause.

Consequences of unclear duration also create problems. Byron, a third grader, is a good example. When he disrupts class, his teacher asks him to go to the time-out area until she feels he's ready to return to his seat.

"How long is that?" Byron wonders. "Five minutes? Ten? Twenty? Possibly all morning?" Byron isn't sure, but he knows one way to find out. Every few minutes he calls out, "Is it time yet?" His annoyed teacher considers adding more time.

Effective consequences have a beginning and an end that are clear and well-defined. Unclear or open-ended consequences invite the type of testing Byron did. If his teacher had specified five minutes as the amount of time Byron needed to spend in time-out, her consequence would have been clear. Byron probably wouldn't have persisted with his disruptive questioning.

Respect

Drake, a sixth grader, enjoys negative attention, and he has discovered a good way to get it. When it's his turn to be blackboard monitor, he runs his fingernails down the center of the board and gets the intended response. His teacher isn't amused.

"Drake, you can erase the board quietly or we can find someone else to do the job. What would you like to do?"

"OK," says Drake with a mischievous smile. "I'll do it the right way." He does, too, for the rest of the morning, but when he's finishing up a job later that afternoon, he runs his fingernail down the board once again.

"Take your seat please, Drake," says his teacher matter-of-factly. She turns to the class. "Who would like to be Drake's replacement for the rest of the week?" A half dozen hands shoot up.

Drake received a clear message about his teacher's rules and expectations. He also received an important object lesson in respectful problem solving. No one was blamed or criticized. No feelings were hurt, and no relationships were damaged.

Now, consider how this situation might have been handled by another teacher who uses the punitive approach. When Drake runs his fingernail down the board the first time, this teacher explodes.

"I knew I couldn't trust you with even a simple task," she says angrily. "You obviously need a few years to grow up before you're ready for this type of responsibility. Now take your seat!" Sure, her consequence stops Drake's misbehavior, but what does he learn in the process?

The method we use is the method we teach. The method itself communicates a message about acceptable behavior. When we apply consequences in hurtful ways, we teach hurtful problem solving.

Clean Slates

It's been three weeks since Kyle, a seventh grader, was suspended from school for instigating a food fight in the cafeteria. He threw a carton of milk and hit another student in the head. Although Kyle has been well behaved in the cafeteria ever since, his fourth-period teacher continues to remind him almost daily about the poor choice he made and the consequence he experienced.

Kyle's teacher can't seem to let go of the consequence. Her focus is stuck on stopping the unacceptable behavior when it should be directed to encouraging Kyle's present cooperation. Kyle needs a clean slate and a fresh opportunity to show that he can make an acceptable choice and behave responsibly.

What You Can Expect

When you begin holding your students accountable with effective consequences, you are likely to encounter an initial increase in testing and resistance. Don't be alarmed. This is temporary. It's a normal part of the learning and retraining process.

Your students have already formed beliefs about how you are supposed to behave based on months and sometimes years of experience. They are not likely to change these well-established beliefs overnight just because you said things are going to be different. They will need to experience more than your words to be convinced.

Imagine how you would react if a close friend told you he was going to behave differently. Let's say this person had always been critical and judgmental of others in the past, and now he claims that he's going to be more tolerant and accepting. Wouldn't you want to see the change for yourself over time before you believed it? Most of us would. Students are the same.

Telling students that you've changed may not be enough to change their beliefs or their behavior. They will want to experience the change for themselves over time before they are likely to revise their beliefs and accept the fact that you are different. You will have to show them with your consistent behavior.

In the meantime, you should expect them to test your new methods and do everything they can to get you to behave "the way you are supposed to." If you've been doing a permissive dance in the past, they will probably continue to ignore you, tune you out, challenge your requests, and dangle delicious baits to get you back out on the dance floor. If you've been punitive, they will probably continue to annoy you and provoke your anger.

Consequences will play an important role during this retraining period. You will probably need to use them frequently. The more hours of consistency you achieve between your words and actions, the quicker your students will learn to tune back in, reduce their testing, and cooperate without the need for consequences.

How long will this take? This depends on a number of factors—the age of your students, your consistency, temperaments, and how much history you and your students need to overcome. Most teachers who apply the methods with good consistency report a significant reduction in testing during the first eight weeks. Younger children, ages three to seven, respond more quickly. Older children and teens require longer. Your consistency will accelerate the learning process for children of all ages.

The notion of a quick fix is very appealing. We all want our students' behavior to improve as quickly as possible, but we also need to recognize that these patterns did not develop overnight. Retraining takes time. Expectations of a quick fix will only set you and your students up for unnecessary frustration and disappointment. Allow the teaching-and-learning process the time it needs to do its part.

Chapter Summary

Consequences can be powerful training tools when used in appropriate ways. They can stop misbehavior. They can teach your rules, and they can promote responsibility by holding children accountable for poor choices and behavior. When applied consistently, consequences define the path you want your students to stay on.

The key to using consequences effectively is the manner in which we apply them. When we apply them in permissive or punitive ways, consequences have limited instructional value. They teach different lessons than we intend, and we end up being responsible for most of the problem solving. When we apply consequences in a democratic manner, however, we can stop misbehavior and teach our rules in the clearest and most understandable way.

Effective consequences share certain properties or characteristics that contribute to their effectiveness. Your consequences will have their greatest impact when they are immediate, consistent, logically related, temporary, respectful, and followed by clean slates. Now that you understand how to get the most guidance value from your consequences, let's move on and examine the different types of consequences available to you.

Chapter

10

Natural Consequences: Natural Learning Experiences

It's snack time in Mrs. Clarey's kindergarten class. She passes out small paper cups filled with nuts and raisins to her students, and they all go outside to eat their snacks on the lawn. Two of her students, Dustin and Max, decide to play a game with their food. They toss their snacks into the air and try to catch them in their mouths. Most ends up on the ground.

"Their snacks won't last long like that," Mrs. Clarey thinks to herself. She's right. Within minutes, the boys come up and ask for more.

"Sorry," she replies. "One cup each is all we get."

Mrs. Clarey let the natural consequence of losing snacks teach the lesson Dustin and Max need to learn. Like many of us, she was probably tempted to say "I told you so" or to provide a lecture on the poor choice of play-ing with their food. She also knew that any further words or actions on her part would take responsibility away from the boys and sabotage their real-life learning experience. Dustin and Max will probably think carefully next time they decide to play that game.

Natural consequences, as the name implies, follow nat-urally from an event or situation. They send the right ac-tion messages to children because they place responsibility where it belongs—on the child. Natural consequences re-quire little or no involvement from teachers. We can easily sabotage the training value of this guidance strategy when we become overinvolved, try to fix the problem, add more consequences, give lectures, or add an "I told you so."

Some teachers find natural consequences easy to use and welcome opportunities to let children learn from their own mistakes. For others, particularly those who oper-ate from the punitive model, natural consequences are not easy to use. When something happens, they have to fight their desire to take charge and control the lesson. Doing nothing when you want to do something can be frustrating.

If you find yourself wanting to take charge and control the lesson, practice limiting your involvement to restating the obvious facts of the situation. For example, if your stu-dents kick the soccer ball onto the roof after you asked them to play away from the building, you might say, "When the ball is on the roof, it's not available to play with." No further words or actions are needed.

Let's look at some of the many situations where you can use natural consequences.

Situations for Using Natural Consequences

1. *When playground equipment or learning materials are lost, damaged, or stolen due to carelessness, misuse, or lack of responsibility.*

Natural consequence: Don't repair or replace the lost or damaged items until enough time has passed for students to experience the loss.

Mr. Ackers, a principal at an inner-city elementary school, loves basketball. He'll do almost anything to encourage his students to play. When the kids ask him to lower the rims on one of the courts so they can stuff the ball through the basket, he is happy to help out.

But Mr. Ackers soon notices a problem. Some kids continue to hang on the rims after they stuff the ball. "The rims won't last long if they keep that up," Mr. Ackers says to himself. When he explains his concern to the kids, they promise to be careful, but many continue to hang on the rims. By the end of the week, one rim is so badly damaged it is unusable. So the kids play half-court games with the remaining lowered rim. It's not long before that one is damaged, too.

"We need new rims to practice stuffing," the kids say the next time they see Mr. Ackers. He recognizes his opportunity to use a natural consequence.

"Rims are expensive," he says. "They don't last long when people hang on them. It will be a while before we can replace them." He wants the kids to experience the loss for several weeks or perhaps a month before he replaces the rims. Next time, they'll probably think twice before hanging on them.

2. *When children make a habit out of forgetting.*

Natural consequence: Don't remind them or take away their responsibility by doing for them what they should do for themselves.

Nine-year-old Kendra has a habit of forgetting her homework and lunch money in the mornings. Each time this occurs, one of her parents drops the forgotten item off at school. Noticing that this had become a pattern,

Kendra's teacher suggests that the parents not make any extra trips for a two-week period.

"Kendra is a good student," says the teacher. "If she misses one or two lunches or assignments, it's not going to hurt her." Her parents agree.

On Tuesday of the first week, Kendra forgets her lunch money. When lunchtime arrives, she asks her teacher if her parents dropped off her lunch money. "Not yet," says her teacher.

That night, Kendra complains to her parents. "You forgot my lunch money! I couldn't eat lunch today."

"I'm sure you'll remember it tomorrow," says her father matter-of-factly. Nothing further was said.

Kendra did remember her lunch money, but on Thursday she left without her homework. Around midmorning she asks her teacher if her parents dropped it off. "Not yet," says her teacher. Kendra received a zero on the assignment.

Once again, she complains to her parents. "You forgot to bring my homework. I got a zero on that assignment!"

"You're a very good student," says her mother. "I'm sure you'll remember it tomorrow." She did.

3. *When children fail to do their part.*

Natural consequence: Let them experience the result.

Austin, a ninth grader, knows he's supposed to take his dirty gym clothes home on Fridays to be washed, but when he opens his locker Monday morning, he sees the bag of dirty clothes. The aroma is unmistakable.

"Oh no!" he says to himself. "What am I going to do?" He decides to present his dilemma to his gym teacher.

"May I be excused from gym class today, Mr. Edwards? I left my gym clothes in my locker over the weekend. They really stink."

Mr. Edwards understands the situation. He also recognizes his opportunity to let the natural consequence teach Austin the lesson he needs to learn.

"Sorry, Austin," says Mr. Edwards matter-of-factly. "There's nothing I can do. You can wear them the way they are or lose half a grade for not dressing. It's up to you." Austin decides to wear them. His classmates give him plenty of room to do his calisthenics. Austin took his gym clothes home that evening. He didn't forget again.

4. *When kids dawdle or procrastinate.*

Natural consequence: When possible, let them experience the consequence of their procrastination.

Michelle, a tenth grader, is a pro at procrastination. Each morning, Monday through Friday, she waits until the last possible moment to get ready for school. After she misses her bus, which she does most of the time, she pleads with her parents for a ride. Reluctantly, one of them bails her out then lectures her about responsibility all the way to school.

"This is crazy!" complains Michelle's mom to her daughter's guidance counselor. "She makes it to school on time, but we end up late."

"What would happen if you and your husband left for work on time without prodding, reminding, or offering Michelle a ride after she misses her bus?" asks the counselor.

"She would miss her bus and have to walk about a mile and a half to school," replies Michelle's mom. "I'm sure she would be late."

"Right," agrees the counselor, "and she would have to pick up a tardy slip at the attendance office before she could be admitted to class. After three tardy slips, she would have to put in an hour of detention. Maybe you should let the natural consequences of her procrastination teach the lesson Michelle needs to learn."

That evening, her parents sat down with Michelle and explained that things were going to be different. "We're not going to prod or remind you anymore in the mornings," said her mom, "and we're not going to bail you out with rides if you miss the bus."

"I'll believe it when I see it," Michelle thinks to herself. She became a believer the next morning. Not a word was said when she went into her usual stall, not even when she missed her bus at 7:30. Her parents left for work on time. At 7:45, Michelle wasn't even dressed. She walked to school and picked up a tardy slip. The second day followed the same pattern, but that's all it took for her to get the message. The third day, she caught her bus and arrived at school on time. Natural consequences helped her make a better choice.

Questions About Natural Consequences

1. *Are poor grades on report cards an effective natural consequence for children who fail to complete their assignments or homework?*

Answer: The answer depends on how much the child values grades. When children value the grades they receive, then low marks can be an instructive natural consequence. When children don't value grades, however, low marks have little impact. You will need to use logical consequences to get the message across.

2. *Several of my students regularly forget to bring their lunches or lunch money to school, and I end up bailing them out by lending them money or calling their parents to arrange a drop-off. This has become a problem. Should I politely refuse to help them the next time they ask, or are there some preparatory steps I should take to ensure the success of the natural consequence?*

Answer: There are several preparatory steps I recommend for handling this type of problem. First, contact the parents, explain the problem, suggest natural consequences as a solution, and request their support. This reduces the likelihood that your natural consequences will be misunderstood or perceived as a punitive measure.

Most parents will be happy to support your plan when they understand what you're trying to achieve.

Second, inform the students that you can't help them out any longer. Now the hot potato is in their lap. All you need to do is allow the consequence to teach its lesson the next time they forget.

3. *I have been consistent about not bailing my students out when they forget homework or lunch money, but some continue to forget. Does this mean natural consequences are ineffective?*

Answer: No. Natural consequences are training tools. Use them as often as necessary to teach the lesson your students need to learn. Some children need to collect a lot of data by learning things the hard way before they arrive at the desired conclusion and change their behavior.

Chapter Summary

Natural consequences follow naturally from an event or situation. They send the right messages to children because they place responsibility where it belongs—on the child. This is learning the hard way. The child is simply allowed the opportunity to experience the outcome of his or her own poor choice or behavior. The process requires little or no involvement from teachers other than not trying to fix the problem. Overinvolvement by adults is one of the surest ways to sabotage the training value of the natural lesson.

Natural consequences can be used in many situations to address a variety of problem behaviors. In some cases, it's best to contact parents prior to using natural consequences. Explain the procedure and request their support. Most will be happy to support you when you understand what you're trying to do.

Chapter

11

Logical Consequences: Structured Learning Experiences

Logical consequences are a highly effective guidance procedure popularized by Rudolf Dreikurs and proponents of Adlerian psychology. Unlike natural consequences that follow naturally from an event or situation, logical consequences are structured learning opportunities. They are arranged by an adult, experienced by the child, and logically related to the situation or misbehavior.

Logical consequences send clear action messages. They stop misbehavior. They teach our rules, and they answer research questions that were not answered with our words. When children experience logical consequences, they know where they stand and what we expect.

Some teachers have difficulty using logical consequences because they are unsure about when to use them or how to set them up. This chapter will show you how to do that. You'll find that logical consequences are easy to use when you think in simple terms and follow some general guidelines. Consider the following example.

It's music time in Mrs. Allen's third-grade class. The kids have been practicing the song "Hot Cross Buns" with their recorders all week. They've nearly mastered it. The practice goes well until Lisa decides to prolong the rehearsal. Each time she reaches a certain point in the song, she blasts away with a high note.

The first time, everyone laughs, even Mrs. Allen. They think it's an accident. The second time, only Lisa laughs. Mrs. Allen gives her some choices.

"Lisa, you can practice the right way, or you'll have to put away your recorder and sit quietly while the rest of us practice. What would you like to do?"

"I'll practice the right way, " says Lisa. The practice resumes. When the class reaches that familiar point in the song, Lisa can't resist. She lets out another high note.

"Put your recorder away, Lisa," says Mrs. Allen matter-of-factly. "You can join us for music again tomorrow."

Lisa's teacher is using a logical consequence to support her rule about cooperating during music. Since Lisa chose not to use her recorder the right way and cooperate with the lesson, she temporarily loses her recorder and the privilege of practicing with the class. The consequence removes some of Lisa's power and control, but not her responsibility. In effect, she chose the consequence she experienced.

Guidelines for Using Logical Consequences

Logical consequences have their greatest impact when they are immediate, consistent, temporary, and followed with a clean slate. The following guidelines should be helpful.

1. *Use your normal voice.*

Logical consequences are most effective when carried out in a matter-of-fact manner with your normal voice. Language that sounds angry, punitive, or emotionally loaded conveys overinvolvement on your part and takes responsibility away from the child. When this occurs, an instructive lesson can backfire into a power struggle and generate resentment. Remember, our goal is to discourage unwanted behavior, not the child performing the behavior.

2. *Think in simple terms.*

Many adults have difficulty using logical consequences because they think too hard and get confused by all the details. The appropriate logical consequence is usually apparent when we think in simple terms. For example, most misbehavior involves at least one of the following circumstances: children with other children, children with adults, children with objects, children with activities, or children with privileges. In most cases, you can apply a logical consequence by temporarily separating one child from another, a child from an adult, a child from an object such as a jump rope, a child from an activity such as a game, or a child from a privilege such as recess or computer use.

3. *Before rules are violated, set up logical consequences with limited choices.*

For example, Glenda, age six, knows she's supposed to keep her hands to herself in the bus line, but the temptation to horse around is great. She reaches over and tugs on the back of Carly's backpack.

"Hey, cut it out!" shouts Carly. The teacher sees what's going on and gives Glenda some choices.

"Glenda, you can keep your place in line if you keep your hands to yourself. If not, you'll have to stand by me at the back of the line. What would you like to do?"

"I'll keep my hands to myself," replies Glenda.

"Good choice," says the teacher.

The teacher in this example intervened early and was able to arrange a logical consequence by giving Glenda limited choices. Glenda received all the information she needed to make an acceptable choice. In this case, she chose to cooperate. If she had decided instead to continue horsing around, the teacher would have followed through and moved her to the back of the line. Either way, Glenda was held accountable for her behavior.

4. *After rules have been violated, apply logical consequences directly.*

Sometimes, we don't arrive on the scene until after our rules have already been violated. In these situations, we should apply our logical consequences directly.

For example, Thad and Byron, two sixth graders, are supposed to be working on a science experiment. Instead, they pinch each other with tweezers from their dissection kits. Their teacher intervenes with logical consequences.

"Put away the tweezers," she says matter-of-factly. "Chad, please sit at the back table for the next ten minutes, and Byron, you can sit in the empty chair next to my desk. You both can have your tweezers back in ten minutes if you use them the right way."

When the teacher arrived on the scene, her rules had already been violated. The time for limited choices had passed. The boys needed a clear action message to stop their misbehavior and reinforce the classroom rules. By separating them from their dissecting tools and each other, she succeeded in teaching the intended lesson.

5. *Use timers for dawdling and procrastinating.*

Timers are useful in situations when children test and resist limits by dawdling or procrastinating. Liz and Becky are a good example. These two fourth graders live for recess. They're usually the first ones out the door when the bell rings and the last ones to return when recess ends. It's the last part that has become a problem, but their teacher has a plan for holding them accountable.

The next time the girls arrive late from recess, their teacher greets them at the door with a stopwatch. She clicks the watch as they walk through the door and announces, "You both owe me forty seconds from your next recess. You can leave forty seconds after everyone else."

Forty seconds may not sound like much of a consequence, but it can be an eternity to two fourth graders who want to be the first ones out the door. After several of these experiences, Liz and Becky started returning to class on time.

6. *Use logical consequences as often as you need them.*

Logical consequences are training tools. Use them as often as needed to stop misbehavior and support your rules. If you need to repeat the same consequence three or more times a day for the same misbehavior, don't be too quick to assume that the consequence is ineffective. More likely, you're dealing with an aggressive researcher who needs to collect a lot of data before he or she will be convinced you mean business. Well-established beliefs and behavior patterns don't change overnight.

Situations for Using Logical Consequences

Logical consequences have instructive applications in a wide variety of situations. The following are just a few of the many possibilities.

189

1. *When children misuse classroom materials, instructional items, or playground equipment.*

Logical consequence: Separate the child from the item temporarily.

Derek, a third grader, knows it's not OK to swing on the tetherball rope but does it anyway and gets caught.

"Stop swinging on the tetherball rope, Derek," says the yard-duty teacher. "You need to find another game to play today. You can try tetherball again tomorrow."

2. *When children make messes.*

Logical consequence: Clean it up.

Todd and Kirk, two seventh graders, write graffiti in the boy's bathroom and get caught. Graffiti has been a serious problem at their school. A lot of money has been spent on cleaning it up. The staff is concerned, but they are divided about the best way to deal with the problem.

The principal wants to send a strong message to other students. He suggests suspending the boys for a week and turning the matter over to the police.

The dean of boys thinks the principal's plan is too harsh. "They need to understand the seriousness of what they did," he says. He recommends eight weeks of mandatory counseling.

The vice principal has another idea. He proposes a logical consequence. "Todd and Kirk helped make the mess. Shouldn't they clean it up?" He suggests giving them some choices. "They can put in forty hours of their own time cleaning up graffiti, or they can be suspended, and the matter can be turned over to the police." Everyone liked the plan.

When the choices were presented to the boys, they decided to avoid the police and put in forty hours of clean up. The lesson wasn't lost on others.

3. *When children are destructive.*

Logical consequence: When possible, have them repair, replace, or pay for the damaged items.

Sondra, a fifth grader, is a determined campaign manager. She'll do almost anything to get her candidate elected including tearing up posters of a rival candidate. She does this and gets caught. The principal calls her to the office.

"I know you want to help your friend, but destroying posters of other candidates isn't the best way to go about it," says the principal. "Sandy is missing fourteen posters. I asked her to give me one to use as a model. You need to bring in fourteen more just like it tomorrow and help her put them up before class."

4. *When children misuse or abuse privileges.*

Logical consequence: Temporary loss or modification of the privilege.

Mr. Peters, a tenth-grade biology teacher, has a liberal policy on giving hall passes, that is, until students take advantage of him. Garrett is one of those students. When he takes nearly fifteen minutes to retrieve something from his locker, Mr. Peters meets him at the door.

"No more hall passes this quarter," says Mr. Peters.

5. *When children won't cooperate with other children.*

Logical consequence: Separate the uncooperative child from others temporarily.

Cleve, a first grader, throws sand at others in the sandbox. When his classmates complain, the yard-duty teacher uses a logical consequence.

"We don't throw sand," says the teacher. "You need to find somewhere else to play this recess. You can play in the sandbox again next recess if you don't throw sand."

6. *When children try to hook us into arguments or treat us disrespectfully.*

Logical consequence: Separate yourself from the child temporarily.

Roberta, a ninth grader, wants to leave class early to get a good seat at a spirit rally. When her teacher denies the request, Roberta does her best to turn a no into a yes.

"Come on, Mr. Richards," pleads Roberta. "Be fair!"

"You'll have plenty of time to get a seat if you leave with everyone else, " he replies.

"Yeah, but not a good seat," argues Roberta. "I don't want to sit in the very back. What's the big deal, anyway?" Her voice has a sarcastic tone. Mr. Richards decides to cut off the discussion.

"We're done talking about it," he says. "If you bring it up again, you'll have to spend some time by yourself."

"Why?" Roberta protests. "Are you afraid you might be wrong?"

"Take your books and have a seat at the back table," says Mr. Richards. "I'll let you know when it's time to rejoin the group." He said the discussion was over, and he backed up his words with a time-out.

7. *When children waste or misuse instructional time.*

Logical consequence: Make up the wasted time.

Kendall, a third grader, has twenty minutes to complete a page of math problems before recess. Fifteen minutes go by. He hasn't done a single one. He hopes to avoid the assignment altogether.

"Put your worksheets on my desk when you're done and line up for recess," says the teacher. Kendall is the first to turn in his assignment. He hopes she won't check his work. She does.

"You're not ready, Kendall," says his teacher matter-of-factly. "Your work isn't finished."

"I'll finish it at home tonight," he says, hoping she'll go for it. She doesn't.

"The assignment is due now," she says. "Since you've chosen not to finish it during class time, you'll have to finish it during recess." Kendall spends his recess completing his worksheet. He'll probably think carefully next time he wants to avoid an assignment.

8. *When children fail to handle activities responsibly.*

Logical consequence: Separate the child from the activity temporarily.

Roy, a fifth grader, knows he's supposed to sit quietly at school assemblies but decides to show off for his friends. His teacher takes him aside.

"Roy, you can sit with your friends if you're quiet. If you're not, I'll have to move you. What would you like to do?"

"I'll be quiet," says Roy, but within minutes, he's talking loudly and being disruptive. His teacher intervenes a second time.

"Roy, you need to sit next to me," she says matter-of-factly.

Consequences with a Cost

Imagine a line that separates two types of consequences: those that place a minimal drain on your time, energy, and resources and those that are costly and require considerable time, planning, and assistance to carry out. Most of the consequences we've examined thus far have been inexpensive. Now, we will cross the line and look at the next group of consequences that carries a higher price tag. Most are familiar procedures used to address extreme or persistent misbehaviors. All can be used as logical consequences, and all require more time, planning, and assistance from others to carry out.

Before using costly procedures, there are some questions we should ask ourselves. First, is the misbehavior severe enough to warrant an expensive consequence? Second, have we exhausted all the less expensive options to resolve the problem?

If the answer to either of these questions is no, then the problem is not being handled at the appropriate level. Responsibility for problem solving is being passed on to others. Expensive consequences should be used judiciously. With this in mind, let's look at some of these expensive, but potentially effective, procedures.

Parent Conferences

Parent conferences can be an effective guidance tool when the parents are customers, that is, when they are willing and able to support us and follow through. But not all parents are customers. Some want to help but can't because they are unavailable or lack the necessary skills. Others want to keep the responsibility for problem solving in the teacher's lap. If you are fortunate enough to work with customers like the teacher in the next example, you face a best-case scenario.

It's the fourth week of school, and Adam, a sixth grader, continues to clown around daily. His teacher has exhausted all of his usual steps to resolve the problem, but the clowning continues. He thinks it's time to arrange a parent conference, but before he does, he discusses the consequence with Adam.

"I try to work out problems with my students before I involve their parents," the teacher begins, "but we haven't made much progress. Do we need some help from your parents?"

Adam wants to avoid this step if possible. He promises things will improve, but the next day, he picks up where he left off. It's as though their conversation never took place. So Adam's teacher follows through and schedules a twenty-minute conference for the following morning before school.

The teacher begins the conference by commenting on Adam's strengths and positive qualities. Then he shares his concerns and the steps he has taken to deal with them.

"How can we help?" asks Adam's father.

"When Adam arrives home with a notice because he spent time outside the classroom for disrupting, please make sure he completes the work he misses. I'll write his missed assignments on the notice."

"We can do more than that," replies Adam's mother. "On the days that Adam has difficulty cooperating, we will set aside an hour after school to practice cooperation. I can think of lots of things I would like some cooperation with." Adam doesn't like the sound of this remedy.

With a solution in place, Adam's teacher thanks the parents and arranges a follow-up conference four weeks later to evaluate Adam's progress. But Adam's behavior improves right away. The conference provided the wake-up call and accountability he needed.

In Adam's case, the conference was effective because his parents were customers and willing to follow through. Their support made the difference. Adam's teacher also helped his own cause by following some general guidelines for effective conferencing. You can, too. The following tips should help.

Guidelines for Conducting Parent Conferences

1. *Be proactive.*

Schedule the conference promptly after you've exhausted your options to resolve the problem at a lower level. No parent likes to hear that a problem has been allowed to continue for a long period of time before he or

195

she is notified or involved. Parents will appreciate your responsiveness.

2. *Include the child in the conference.*

The fact that the parents and teacher are working together sends a strong message to the child: "We care, and we will work together to hold you accountable." Sometimes the message is lost when the child is excluded from the conference.

3. *Be positive.*

You can create the right climate for problem solving by beginning the conference with a positive statement or anecdote about the child such as "Jana is a real helper in the classroom" or "I know I can count on Greg's leadership on the playground." A positive start helps parents relax and become more receptive to what follows.

4. *Keep the conference focused.*

Sometimes conferences ramble or lose their focus because the parents and teacher do not share the same agenda. The best way to tackle the problem of hidden or competing agendas is to state the purpose and goals for the conference at the outset as well as your time constraints. Ask the parents if they have any additional issues they would like to discuss and, if needed, schedule a follow-up call or conference. When parents realize that their concerns will be addressed, they're less likely to interrupt or steer the conference in other directions.

5. *Come prepared to offer solutions.*

No parent likes to have a problem dumped in his or her lap or to be put on the spot to come up with a quick solution. Come to the conference prepared to offer a solution or a back-up plan in the event your solution is not feasible. If the solution to the problem is not clear, be prepared to direct the parents to the appropriate resources for assistance such as counseling, a professional evaluation, helpful books, or parenting classes.

6. *Schedule a follow-up conference to evaluate progress.*
Follow-up conferences demonstrate commitment and build accountability into the process.

On-Campus Suspension (OCS)

Some misbehaviors such as extreme defiance, disruption, or injurious behavior require removing students from the classroom for more than brief periods of time. In these situations, on-campus suspension can be an effective consequence.

Darrell, an eighth grader, knows it's not OK to wear hats in the classroom but decides to challenge the school rule and do it anyway. He arrives at his first-period class with his hat on and waits for the teacher to ask him to take it off. When she does, he explodes.

"Buzz off!" he shouts. "I don't have to follow your stupid rules or take any crap from you or anybody else." He slumps back in his chair defiantly.

"Pick up your books and take them with you to OCS, Darrell," says the teacher matter-of-factly. "You can join us again tomorrow." She hands him a slip with the time on it and sends him to the on-campus suspension center for the rest of the period.

Darrell was hoping his protest would be his ticket home for the day. When he arrives at OCS, he decides to stick with his original plan and keeps his hat on.

"You know the rules, Darrell," says the OCS supervisor. "If you don't take it off, I'll have to send you to the vice principal's office. He'll probably send you home for the day."

"Go ahead. Make my day," Darrell says to himself. He knows his parents can't afford to take any time away from work. He'd love to spend his day hanging out at the mall. He leaves his hat on.

When Darrell arrives at the office, the vice principal has a good idea about what's going on. He gives Darrell some choices. "You can spend the rest of the period in OCS with your hat off or you can spend the rest of the day in OCS with it on. What would you like to do?"

These were not the choices Darrell expected. He takes a moment to consider what his day would be like in OCS. No visiting with friends between classes or during lunch. None of his usual privileges. He would eat lunch by himself, take periodic bathroom breaks, and spend most of his day catching up on assignments from his various classes. Reluctantly, Darrell takes off his hat and heads to OCS for the rest of first period.

As the example illustrates, on-campus suspension has many advantages. It stops the immediate misbehavior. It removes the audience and payoffs for misbehavior. And it maintains the student in an instructional setting to the greatest extent possible. The message to Darrell was clear: You will stay at school. You can cooperate in class and enjoy your usual privileges and the company of your peers, or you can work quietly by yourself without your peers or privileges. The best option was not difficult to figure out.

Although OCS is best suited for larger schools with a high incidence of misbehavior, the procedure can be adapted for smaller schools. The procedure is flexible. Some schools use OCS as a second-stage time-out area.

The primary disadvantage of OCS is cost. An on-campus suspension center is expensive to operate. It requires a full-time staff position to supervise students, an available classroom, and a set of record-keeping procedures to track referrals, arrivals, departures, and no-shows. The following guidelines will help you set up an on-campus suspension program.

Guidelines for Operating OCS

1. *Select an appropriate place for OCS.*

The room should be large enough for students to sit well apart from one another.

2. *Provide work folders.*

OCS should be a quiet place for students to work. Referring teachers should send work folders along with their students.

3. *Adapt the procedure if necessary.*

Elementary schools or schools with a low incidence of extreme misbehavior can adapt the procedure by using it as the second stage of a two-stage time-out procedure described in the following chapter.

4. *Hold no-shows accountable.*

Students who fail to show up for OCS should make up the missed time in after-school detention, Saturday school, or experience a similar consequence.

5. *Hold referring teachers accountable.*

OCS referral forms should include a section for the teacher to complete indicating all prior steps taken to resolve the problem. The referral should clearly indicate that OCS is an appropriate consequence for the student's misbehavior.

Saturday School

Saturday school is an effective logical consequence at the secondary level for handling problems with tardies, cuts, or truancy. The message is clear: Make up the time you missed. Although the program requires costly supervision, room space, and record keeping, much of the costs can be recovered through the additional aid generated by student attendance.

The biggest disadvantage of Saturday school is that the consequence cannot be enforced without parent support. When parents are willing to hold their children accountable, a day or two of Saturday school can be very instructive. Consider the following:

Julie and Miranda, both ninth graders, decide to hang out at the mall during the first three periods of their day. When they arrive at their fourth-period classes, they are called to the attendance office.

"May I see the excuse notes from your parents so I can admit you to class?" asks the attendance clerk. Neither girl has a note or a good excuse. The clerk alerts the vice principal, who gives the girls some choices.

"You both will have to make up your truancies with half a day of Saturday school. There are two Saturdays left in the month. Which one would you like?" Julie and Miranda both know their parents will support the consequence. They'll probably think carefully next time they consider spending class time at the mall.

After-School Detention

After-school detention is another logical consequence for handling problems such as tardies or wasted time. As Nick discovers in the following example, the procedure provides accountability for those students who want to move on to more pleasurable activities at the end of their day.

Nick, a seventh grader, arrives late for class for the third time during the semester. When he goes to the attendance office to pick up a tardy slip, he's informed that he must put in one hour of after-school detention that afternoon as a consequence.

"What a drag!" Nick says to himself. "I was planning to go Rollerblading with my friends." After-school detention gave Nick a new reason for arriving at class on time.

Off-Campus Suspension

As a guidance tool, off-campus suspension shares the same limitation as parent conferences. The success of the procedure depends upon cooperation between home and school. The school can exclude a student from campus, but it has no control over what happens when the student leaves. Enforcing the consequence is the parents' job. The parents must be customers for the consequence to be effective.

When parents aren't customers, many students view the suspension as a vacation day and welcome opportunities for more. In effect, the consequence becomes a reward for continued misbehavior. When parents are customers, such as the one in the following example, off-campus suspension can be instructive.

Chase, a third grader, decides to play a joke on the girl sitting in front of him. As she begins to sit down, he pulls out her chair, and she falls backward. The joke isn't funny. She has a gash on the back of her head that probably requires stitches.

The teacher asks Chase to collect his books and assignments and sends him to the office with a note. The principal promptly calls his parents and informs them that Chase has been suspended from school for the rest of the day.

"How can we help him learn from this experience?" asks Chase's mom. The principal offers some helpful tips.

"Suspensions are most effective when children spend a quiet day in the house without the privileges they would normally enjoy. No TV, video games, riding bikes, playing in the neighborhood, or hanging out with friends, at least not during school hours. They should spend their time catching up on missed schoolwork, reading, or doing other quiet activities. Tomorrow, Chase can return to school with a clean slate."

In this case, cooperation between home and school ensured the success of the procedure. The off-campus suspension provided Chase with the instructive lesson he needed.

What to Do When Your Consequences Don't Work

Sometimes children don't respond to our logical consequences the way we expect, and we wonder what went wrong. We can usually determine what went wrong and correct the problem by referring back to our list of characteristics of effective consequences. When your students don't respond as expected, check yourself out on the following.

1. *Was your consequence immediate?*

That is, did you apply it soon after the student misbehaved?

2. *Was the consequence applied in a consistent manner?*

That is, did you do what you said you would? Did you do the same thing the last time the student behaved this way and the time before?

3. *Was the consequence logically related to the misbehavior?*

4. *Did you role-model the type of problem solving you intended?*

Consequences are less effective when applied in a punitive or permissive manner.

5. *Was the consequence temporary in duration?*

Did it have a clear beginning and an end? When you said it was over, was it really over? Or did you add an "I told you so" at the end?

6. *Was the consequence followed by a clean slate and forgiveness?*

Chapter Summary

Logical consequences are structured learning experiences. They are arranged by the adult, experienced by the child, and logically related to the event or misbehavior. Logical consequences send clear action messages children really understand. They stop misbehavior. They support our rules, and they answer questions that were not answered with our words.

Logical consequences are easy to use if we think in simple terms and follow some general guidelines. Most incidents of misbehavior involve at least one of the following circumstances: children with other children, children with adults, children with objects, children with activities, or children with privileges. In most cases, we can apply a logical consequence by temporarily separating one child from another, a child from an adult, a child from an object (such as a toy), a child from an activity (such as a game), or a child from a privilege (such as recess).

Often before your rules are violated, you can set up your logical consequences with limited choices. After your rules have been violated, apply logical consequences directly. Logical consequences are training tools. Use them as often as needed.

Chapter

12

Time-Out: A Stop Signal Children Understand

Cassie, age three, sits on the floor building a tower with blocks when the boy sitting next to her accidentally bumps her. "Move!" shouts Cassie angrily. "You almost knocked over my tower." When the boy doesn't move, Cassie gets up and kicks him in the back. He screams. The teacher intervenes.

"Cassie, please sit by yourself at the back table for a while," says her teacher matter-of-factly. "I'll set the timer for three minutes." When the time is over, Cassie and her teacher explore other ways to get people to move without kicking.

In another classroom, Mitch, a sixth grader, tries to spice up a social studies lesson with some live entertainment. While his teacher writes at the board, Mitch pretends to conduct an orchestra. He gets a few laughs. The teacher catches a glimpse of what's going on.

"Have a seat please, Mitch," says the teacher matter-of-factly. Mitch sits down, but he isn't finished yet. He got a few laughs earlier, and he's hungry for more. When the teacher returns to the board, Mitch jumps up once again and begins conducting. More laughter. This time, the teacher decides to put a little distance between Mitch and his audience.

"Take your books and have a seat at the back table, Mitch," says the teacher. "You can join us again in ten minutes." He sets the timer. Mitch heads to the back table.

Mitch is quiet for a few minutes then renews his quest for attention. He drums on the table loud enough to distract others. This time, the teacher decides to completely separate Mitch from his audience.

"Pick up your books and take them with you to Mrs. Currier's class," says the teacher. "You can join us again in twenty minutes." Mitch heads off to Mrs. Currier's room. He won't find a receptive audience there. She teaches second grade.

Both teachers in the previous examples are using time-out. Cassie's teacher used a one-stage procedure to support her rule about kicking. Mitch's teacher needed a two-stage procedure to stop Mitch's persistent disruptiveness. In this chapter, you'll learn how to use both of these procedures to handle a variety of challenging misbehaviors. You'll learn how to set up time-outs, how to carry them out, and how to overcome the obstacles teachers confront with these procedures.

Effective Use of Time-Out

Time-out is an effective guidance tool when used as it was intended—as a logical consequence. The consequence sends all the right signals to children. It stops their misbehavior. It removes their audience and payoffs for disruption, and it helps children restore self-control quickly so they can return to instruction. The procedure is easy to carry out and can be used at all grade levels—preschool, elementary, even secondary school.

Unfortunately, time-out has received some unfavorable press because the procedure has been so widely misused and misunderstood. Those who operate from the punitive model have used it as a jail sentence to force children into submission. The punitive version of time-out sounds something like this: "You sit in the corner and don't leave until I tell you to. I don't want to hear a peep out of you." Punitive time-outs can be quite lengthy, several hours or even days, and they are often carried out in an atmosphere of anger or upset.

On the other extreme, those who operate from the permissive model view time-out as a tool for the child to use at his or her discretion. The child decides when it starts, when it ends, or whether it even happens at all. The permissive version of time-out sounds something like this: "I think it would be a good idea if you take some quiet time by yourself for a while at the back table, OK? You can rejoin the group when you're ready." The child decides the length of time, which is usually quite brief.

In actuality, neither of those methods is really time-out. Time-out is not jail, nor is it an optional consequence for students to use at their own discretion. When time-out is used in either of these ways, responsibility shifts in the wrong direction, and most of the training value of the consequence is lost.

Time-out is really time away from reinforcement. In most classrooms, reinforcement consists of the many rewards of daily routines such as being a member of the group, enjoying full privileges, participating in group activities, getting recognition and attention from others, and enjoying the freedom that goes with cooperation.

Does time-out still sound like jail? The two are similar to the extent that both provide a solid set of walls to stop misbehavior and remove reinforcement. There are also some major differences.

Time-outs are generally brief (three to twenty minutes), whereas jail sentences are quite lengthy. There are few, if any, opportunities for children to practice responsible corrective behavior in jail. Corrective training and learning do not happen there. Time-outs, on the other hand, are brief and can be used repeatedly. There are many opportunities for practicing corrective behavior. Unlike jail, time-out succeeds at teaching the lessons we're trying to get across.

Guidelines for Using Time-Out

Time-out is a quick, simple, and easy-to-carry-out procedure that can be used with students of all grade levels (preschool through secondary) and in many different situations. The procedure is most effective when presented firmly and matter-of-factly as a logical consequence. The following guidelines should be helpful.

1. *Select an appropriate time-out area.*

Selection of an appropriate place for time-out is critical to the success of the procedure. The ideal place within the classroom is an unoccupied partitioned area with four walls, a door, and a window for supervision. Unfortunately, most classroom teachers do not have access to ideal places for time-out, but they can adapt the procedure and use what's always available—their own classrooms and the classrooms of other teachers. The best place within the classroom for time-out is an unoccupied desk, table, or three-sided study carrel positioned away from others near the periphery of the classroom.

Is the school office a suitable place for time-out? Generally not. The school office is a hub of activity with busy people and lots of interesting things going on. For many students, time-out in the office is like watching their own personal soap opera. The consequence is actually a reward. Remember, time-out should be time away from reinforcement. You won't accomplish your purpose if you send a disruptive child to an entertaining area.

Some teachers send students outside the classroom to sit in the hallway for time-out. Is this a recommended practice? Time-outs in the hallway have several disadvantages. The procedure removes students from instruction, often needlessly, and the hallway creates problems with supervision. Most students can take time-out in the classroom without isolating them from instruction and without compromising your duty to keep them supervised. For those students who need more, the two-stage procedure is a better way to go.

Can time-out be used outside the classroom in settings such as the cafeteria, library, or playground? Yes. Select a chair, a bench, or some comfortable spot away from other children. Then keep track of the time.

2. *Use a two-stage procedure for persistent disruption.*

What should you do when students continue to disrupt while in time-out? I recommend using a two-stage time-out procedure such as the one Mitch's teacher used in the opening example. A two-stage procedure is ideal for aggressive researchers like Mitch because it provides escalating consequences for escalating misbehavior. Each stage further removes the disruptive child from his or her audience and from the payoffs for misbehavior. Each stage also provides more time for the child to restore self-control.

The procedure is very simple. Stage one time-outs take place in the child's immediate classroom for a predetermined period of time. Most students will decide to cooperate at this point. A few, like Mitch, may decide to test, and when they do, you'll need a back-up area outside your classroom for time-out. Stage two time-outs should take place in a buddy teacher's classroom for twice the usual period of time. If your school has a supervised on-campus suspension center (OCS), that location is an excellent choice as a second-stage time-out area.

When choosing a buddy teacher, select someone who is familiar with the procedure and who is willing to carry it out in a firm, matter-of-fact manner. The ideal buddy teacher is someone with older or younger students to eliminate the possibility of a receptive audience.

The buddy teacher's job is to provide a place for the child to sit during time-out, to supervise the child, and to keep track of time. This is not a time for interrogation ("What did you do this time?") or shaming ("Oh no, not you again!"), nor should it be a rewarding or pleasurable experience. If the child cooperates during the time-out, the usual outcome, then he or she returns to class when the time is over.

3. *Introduce time-out to your students before using it.*

You can prevent a lot of testing, resistance, and confusion if you introduce the time-out procedure to your students before using it, preferably during the first few days of school. Pose some hypothetical situations and walk your students through the complete procedure so they can see how it works. Consider the following sample introduction from an intermediate teacher to the class.

"I use the time-out procedure when someone disrupts class. Here's how it works. If I think you are unaware of your behavior, I will usually give you a warning such as 'Jimmy, you need to work quietly now,' so you can stop what you are doing. If you continue to disrupt, or if I'm sure you are aware of what you are doing, I will ask you to go to the time-out area. You can take your books and follow along with the lesson or just sit quietly. When the time-out is over, I will ask you to return to your seat. If you leave the area before the time-out is over, you'll have to go back and the time will start over.

"If you continue to disrupt while in time-out, I will ask you to go to Mrs. Smith's class (buddy teacher) for twice the time. You can bring your books and work quietly when you're there or just sit quietly. She will let you know when the time-out is over and you can return to class. Any questions about how time-out works?"

4. *Use a timer.*

Time-outs should always have a beginning and an end that is clear to all involved. Open-ended, vague, or arbitrary time limits such as "You can return when I think you're ready" or "Go to the time-out area for a while" set up both teacher and students for further testing and power struggles.

The best way to keep track of time is to use a time-out timer available through educational supply catalogues. A kitchen timer with an inoffensive chime works fine. I don't recommend relying on wrist watches, wall clocks, or other imprecise measures or permitting your students to set the timer or control the time. Teachers who use this practice discover that time-outs in their classroom are very brief. Once you set the timer, you effectively take yourself out of the picture. The remaining part is between the child and the timer.

How long should time-outs be? One minute per each year of age is a good rule of thumb for preschoolers (for example, four minutes for a four year old). Stage one time-outs should be five to ten minutes for primary level students (kindergarten through grade three) and ten to fifteen minutes for intermediate (grades three through six) and secondary students (grades seven through twelve). Stage two time-outs should be twice as long as stage one time-outs for each respective group.

Keep one additional factor in mind when determining the appropriate length of time for time-out. In all cases, time-outs should be long enough for the child to restore self-control. For example, if a five year old continues to tantrum for twenty minutes before he regains self-control, then that's how long he needs to spend in time-out.

5. *For limit testing, set up time-out with limited choices.*

Lindsey, a second grader, knows she's supposed to keep her hands to herself in the classroom but decides to tickle her neighbor. Her teacher notices and gives Lindsey some choices.

"Lindsey, you can keep your hands to yourself or you can take five minutes at the back table to get yourself under control. What would you like to do?" Her choices are clear. Lindsey decides to cooperate.

Brad, a seventh grader, whistles while he's supposed to be working quietly on a writing assignment. The noise disturbs others. His teacher asks him to stop, and he does briefly, but starts up again a short time later.

"Brad, you need to work on your assignment quietly at the back table," says his teacher matter-of-factly. Brad picks up his papers and heads to the back table for a ten-minute time-out, but within a minute, he whistles again. This time, his teacher gives him some choices.

"Brad, you can work quietly for ten minutes at the back table or you can go next door to Mr. Jacob's room for twenty minutes. What would you like to do?"

"I'll finish up here," replies Brad. He doesn't have any friends in Mr. Jacob's class.

Brad was testing. When he found the wall he was looking for, he made the right choice and cooperated. When you encounter limit testing, you can usually set up a first- or second-stage time-out consequence with limited choices as Brad's teacher did.

6. *When rules have been violated, apply time-out directly.*

Evan, a kindergartner, wants to play with the new hula hoop his teacher brought to class. When the bell rings for morning recess, he races out to find it, but Carly is already playing with it.

· "Hey, I was going to play with that!" shouts Evan when he sees Carly with the toy. He tries to wrestle it away from her, but Carly holds on tight. The struggle continues until Evan decides to bite her on the arm. She screams.

"He bit me," sobs Carly when the teacher comes to investigate. Evan looks remorseful.

"She wouldn't give me the hula hoop," Evan replies.

"We don't bite," says the teacher matter-of-factly. "You need to sit down next to the wall for five minutes. We'll talk about other ways to share the hula hoop when the time is over."

When Evan's teacher arrived on the scene, her rule about biting had already been violated. The time for limited choices had passed. Evan needed to experience the consequence associated with his poor choice. Time-out achieved this purpose effectively.

7. *After the time-out, provide a clean slate.*

When the timer goes off, the consequence should be over, provided the child has stopped misbehaving and is under control. If the child throws a tantrum or is not under control, then he or she is not ready to come out. You can say, "The timer went off. You can leave the time-out area when you're calmed down but not before that time."

When the child is ready to come out, invite him or her back in a friendly voice. Try to resist the temptation to add an "I told you so" or a lecture that personalizes the lesson and sabotages the effectiveness of the consequence.

8. *Hold children accountable for time missed from class.*

When children disrupt to the point that they need to be removed from class, their behavior should be seen as a red flag. Parents should be alerted. If the behavior develops into a pattern, you'll need parental assistance.

213

The notification form shown in Figure 12A is one simple method to keep parents informed. Send the form home with students after school on the days that they require a second-stage time-out. Parents are asked to sign the form and return it with their child the next day.

Figure 12A. Parent notification form

Mrs. Deaver

Date: _____

Room #22   Notice# _____

   This is to inform you that _____

missed _____ minutes of class time today

because he/she continued to disrupt the class

after being asked to stop. The problem was

handled at school and no further assistance

is required at this time.

   Please indicate that you received this

notice by signing and returning it with your

child tomorrow. If you have any questions,

please call. Thank you.

_____
Parent signature   Date

Inform your students that you will follow up with a phone call if the signed notice is not returned.

9. *Use time-out as often as you need it.*

Time-out is a training tool that promotes children's learning when used consistently and appropriately. Don't assume the procedure is ineffective when students persist in their testing or continue to violate your rules. More likely, they need to collect more data to arrive at the conclusions you intend. Consistent repeated exposure to your consequences should lead to the learning you desire.

When to Use Time-Out

Time-out can be used in a variety of settings such as the classroom, playground, library, or cafeteria to address a variety of misbehaviors referred to as "target behaviors." In classroom settings, most target behaviors fall under the general category of disruptive behavior or those behaviors that interfere with your classroom routines, procedures, or the teaching and learning of others. The following are some of the many target behaviors you can address with time-out.

Attention-Seeking Behavior Martin, age four, loves attention—any kind of attention. While his teacher reads a story about farm animals, Martin makes the sound for each animal in the story. His teacher asks him to stop, and he does, for a while, until she comes to the part about pigs. Then he lets out a series of grunts and snorts.

"Take a seat at the back table, Martin," says his teacher matter-of-factly. "It's not OK to interrupt while I'm reading." She sets the timer for five minutes. Martin loses his audience.

Limit-Testing Behavior Buz, a fifth grader, is told he cannot use his skateboard on the playground during school

215

hours, but tries his best to wear his teacher down and turn a no into a yes. "Come on, Mr. Easton," Buz pleads. "I'm not going to get hurt. I know how to use it safely."

"You know the rules, Buz," replies Mr. Easton. "No skateboards on the playground during school hours."

"Well, they're stupid rules," says Buz, "and I don't see why I have to follow them."

"We're done talking about it," says Mr. Easton, realizing the futility of further discussion. "If you bring it up again, you'll have to spend some time by yourself." Buz won't let go.

"Why can't we make an exception, just this once?" asks Buz, looking for a little bargaining room. "I'll even wear my bike helmet and elbow pads." Mr. Easton doesn't take the bait. He's done as much as he can with his words. Now it's time for Buz to experience stopping.

"Have a seat at the back table, Buz. I'll let you know when ten minutes are over."

Disrespectful Behavior Rita, a tenth grader, is unhappy with her teacher for not granting her a deadline extension on a term paper. "You're so unfair!" complains Rita. "Other teachers help students out when they are in a bind. Why can't you?"

"Sorry, Rita," says Mr. Simmons. "You've had a month. I can't give you any more. It's not fair to the others."

"You are so tight!" says Rita with a biting tone to her voice. "What do you care, anyway? You probably get your thrills making life miserable for your students."

"Have a seat at the back table, Rita," says Mr. Simmons matter-of-factly. "I'll let you know when fifteen minutes are up."

"Oh, that really hurts," says Rita sarcastically. "What happens if I don't go to the back table?" she taunts.

Mr. Simmons gives her some choices. "You can go to the back table for fifteen minutes or you can spend the rest of the period at the on-campus suspension center. What would you like to do?"

Rita lets out a big huff. Reluctantly, she heads to the back table.

Defiant Behavior The kids are lined up to go out for recess when Mrs. Lopez notices that one of her second graders has left his art materials all over his desk. "Gregory, you need to put away your art materials before you can go out for recess," says Mrs. Lopez.

"I'll do it when I get back," he says insistently.

"No," she replies. "You can't leave until it's done."

"Well, I'm not going to do it!" says Gregory, crossing his arms. Mrs. Lopez gives him some choices.

"You can pick up the items on your desk or you can spend the next five minutes at the back table getting ready to do it. What would you like to do?" Gregory glares at her and marches to the back table to sit down. After five minutes, the buzzer rings.

"The time is over," Mrs. Lopez announces. "Are you ready to clean up your desk so you can go outside?"

"I'm still not doing it!" says Gregory as defiantly as before.

"That's up to you," says Mrs. Lopez. She gets up to reset the timer, but Gregory has a sudden change of heart.

"OK," he says, realizing the firmness of her resolve. He picks up quickly and tries to salvage what's left of his recess.

Antagonistic or Hurtful Behavior Brenda, an eighth grader, goes to the board to write out a solution to a math problem. She seems unsure. When it's time to go over her work, the teacher finds an error. Brenda looks embarrassed. A classmate does his best to make her feel even worse.

"Nice try, Brenda," says Mark sarcastically. "You only missed it by a hundred." The teacher intervenes.

"Have a seat at the back table, Mark," says the teacher matter-of-factly. "It's not OK to treat anybody like that in this classroom." Mark heads to the back table for a fifteen-minute time-out.

Violent and Aggressive Behavior Brett and George, both sixth graders, get into a heated argument as they head out to the playground. They yell at each other and call each other names. When the yard-duty teacher arrives on the scene, the boys are wrestling on the blacktop with a crowd of students cheering them on. Brett's shirt is ripped, and George has a scratch on his forehead. Both are upset.

"Get up, guys," says the teacher.

"He pushed me first," says George.

"But you called me an asshole," counters Brett.

"You both need to spend fifteen minutes by yourselves," says the teacher, "then we'll talk about other ways to handle the situation." She directs the boys to separate benches at opposite ends of the playground. When the fifteen minutes are up, she calls them over to discuss other ways to resolve their differences without fighting.

Tantrums Shelly, age five, is accustomed to getting her own way at home. When she hears no, Shelly has a proven strategy for turning it into yes. She throws a tantrum. Her parents usually give in. Things are different in Shelly's kindergarten class.

"Recess is over," announces Shelly's teacher. "It's time to come inside." One by one, the kids file back into the classroom, that is, everyone except Shelly. She continues to play on the monkey bars.

"Shelly, you need to come in, too," says the teacher.

"But I'm not ready to come in," says Shelly insistently. "I want to play some more."

"You can play next recess, but now you need to join the class," replies her teacher. Shelly doesn't move. So her teacher takes Shelly's hand, and together, they begin to walk back to class.

"What's going on?" Shelly thinks to herself. This isn't how it's supposed to work." As they near the classroom, she decides to play her trump card. She throws a tantrum. She plops herself down outside the door and begins to cry. "I won't do it!" she sobs.

"That's up to you," says her teacher. "You can join us in five minutes if you're done crying." She sets the timer and asks a parent volunteer to watch Shelly during the time-out.

Shelly is still crying when the buzzer goes off. Fifteen minutes go by, and Shelly is still crying. Finally, twenty minutes after the tantrum began, Shelly walks back into the classroom.

"Hi, Shelly," says the teacher in a friendly voice. "Have a seat." The tantrum didn't work. Next recess, Shelly returns to class with everyone else.

Questions About Time-Out

1. *What should I do when students refuse to go to the time-out area?*

Answer: This is probably further limit testing to determine if you will really follow through or an extreme act of defiance. In either event, you should set up the next consequence by giving the student some limited choices. For example, you might say, "You can go to the time-out area as you were asked, or you can go to the office and work it out with the principal or your parents. What would you like to do?" Give the child twenty to thirty seconds to think it over, then follow through based on his or her decision. If this is an extreme act of defiance, you will probably need assistance from others.

219

2. *What should I do when students leave the time-out area before their time-out is over?*

Answer: Again, this is probably further limit testing. State firmly that they must stay in the time-out area until the full time elapses. If they leave before the time-out is over, ask them to return to the time-out area and start the time over again.

3. *What should I do when students yell and scream while in time-out?*

Answer: This sounds like a tantrum or it may be a discharge of pent-up anger and frustration. Do not reward the tantrum by giving in to it or by resorting to threats, lectures, or other forms of coercion. It's time to move on to a second-stage time-out outside the classroom.

4. *What should I do when students knock over chairs or other items while in time-out?*

Answer: When you introduce the time-out procedure to your class at the beginning of the year, inform them that if they make a mess while in time-out, they will have to clean it up before they leave. A little prevention goes a long way. Remove breakable items from your time-out area.

5. *When I ask some students to go to the time-out area, they mumble, grumble, or talk back disrespectfully as they go there. Should I add five minutes each time they do this?*

Answer: No. That's probably what they want you to do, and if you play it out to the fullest extent, your time-outs will become jail. These students are doing their best to incite a power struggle and get you back out on the dance floor. As tempting as the bait might be, don't bite. If they go to the time-out area and stay there the full time without further disruption, then your time-out procedure is working. If they use obscenities or disrupt during stage one, then move on to stage two. Your students will realize there are no advantages to escalation.

6. *What are students supposed to do while in time-out?*

Answer: The purpose of time-out is to stop the immediate misbehavior and help children restore self-control. There are a number of things children can do in the time-out area to achieve this purpose. You may want to present these options as choices. For example, you might say, "You can bring your book and assignment and follow along with the lesson, or you can just sit there quietly." Some teachers set out *Weekly Readers* or other reading material in the time-out area to help disruptive children settle down and restore self-control. If you provide nothing for an angry or upset child to do while in time-out, you increase the likelihood of further disruption.

7. *What should I do when I ask a student to go to my buddy teacher's classroom for a second-stage time-out and I suspect he or she may not go there directly, if at all?*

Answer: Select a responsible student in your classroom to be an escort. Escorts are an effective way to ensure that children arrive at their destination. Or, if they don't, the escort can inform you quickly so you can notify the office or take other steps to intervene.

8. *Secondary students sometimes try to defeat the two-stage procedure by not showing up at the buddy teacher's class or on-campus suspension center (OCS). How should we deal with this problem?*

Answer: Referring teachers should routinely follow up with their buddy teacher or OCS supervisor to verify compliance. No shows should be held accountable for making up the time in after-school detention or Saturday school. It doesn't take too many of these experiences to increase compliance with the two-stage procedure.

9. *How much disruption is too much? When is it time to use more than time-out as a consequence?*

Answer: Tolerance for disruption varies from teacher to teacher. Some teachers consider two or three disruptive incidents a week to be excessive for any student. Others can tolerate ten or more incidents a week if they see a general pattern of improvement.

If you use the two-stage time-out procedure consistently for four to six weeks and experience only minimal reduction in disruptive behavior, then it's time to investigate the underlying causes for the behavior and consider other guidance steps. In the next chapter, we'll examine guidance strategies for your most disruptive students.

Chapter Summary

Time-out is a stop signal children really understand. It stops their misbehavior. It removes their audience and other payoffs for misbehavior, and it helps children restore self-control quickly so they can rejoin the class. The consequence is an inexpensive solution for costly behavior problems.

Time-out also is a versatile guidance tool. It can be used in a variety of situations with children of nearly all ages, preschool through secondary. For most students, a one-stage procedure is sufficient to stop their misbehavior and restore their self-control. Your aggressive researchers may require a two-stage procedure that provides escalating consequences for escalating misbehavior. Each stage further separates the disruptive child from his or her audience and from the payoffs for misbehavior.

▼

Chapter

13

Solving Problems with Homework

One of the most familiar dances I see in my counseling work is the dance parents and children do over homework. That's the one where the parents remind, cajole, threaten, and reprimand, and the kids avoid, make excuses, resist, dawdle, or procrastinate. Like most dances, there's a punitive version that's a little louder and a permissive version that's more drawn out. Some parents do a little of both.

Call them "homework battles," "nightly coercion routines," or whatever term you want, one thing is for sure: There are a lot of parents out there doing it. Most can't say how they got started or what keeps it going, but once it gets started, no one seems to know how to stop. Where can parents turn for help? Hopefully, to you. This chapter will show you how to help parents end their homework dances and put the responsibility for homework back on their child's shoulders where it belongs.

Many parents don't realize that homework takes place in a system involving three participants: parents, teacher, and child. Each has his or her own set of jobs or responsibilities to carry out if the homework system is to operate smoothly and remain in balance. The system can break down, and often does, when its members do less than or more than their own part.

In this chapter, you'll learn how the homework system operates, why it breaks down, and how to fix it without returning to the nightly coercion routine. You'll see that the key to a successful homework system is helping parents do their own part, and only their part, without taking responsibility away from you or their child.

The Dance

Darren, a fourth grader, and his parents were referred during the middle of the school year. The problem was Darren wouldn't do his homework. He was failing many of his subjects.

Darren's teacher had tried everything—deadline extensions, extra-credit makeup opportunities, stickers, contracts, success charts, pep talks . . . even a daily note system between school and home. Nothing worked.

Yes, homework sounded like the problem, but was it really? Each year, I see a few kids like Darren for whom homework appears to be the problem but turns out to be only a symptom of something larger, such as a lack of skills, a learning disability, a behavior problem, an emotional or relationship problem, or a problem with drugs or alcohol. I needed to check this out. I interviewed Darren's parents and collected the necessary background information.

From the interview, Darren seemed like a normal, well-adjusted kid. He spent his free time with friends, and he enjoyed skateboarding and bicycling. Other than the power struggles over homework, he enjoyed good relationships with his parents and others. I needed to be sure, however, that Darren was really capable of doing his work.

"Is there any chance that the assignments might be too difficult for him?" I asked.

His parents were prepared for the question. Darren's mother handed me an envelope with copies of past report cards and test scores. I glanced over them briefly. Mostly Bs. Strong test scores. OK, I was convinced. Darren was capable. Back to homework matters.

Darren's parents had all the familiar complaints: "He tells us he doesn't have any homework, then we find out later that he does. He knows he's supposed to write down his assignments, but half the time he doesn't do it. When we ask to see them, he says he forgot or lost them or that he doesn't have any that night. So, we get on the phone and call around and find out what's going on. Some nights, it takes us forty-five minutes just to figure out what his assignments are! Fortunately, that has changed. Now his teacher calls me every Monday and gives me all of Darren's homework assignments for the week."

"Has that helped?" I directed the question to Darren's mother who was telling most of the story.

"Yes and no," she replied. "At least now we know what he's supposed to do, but getting him to actually do it hasn't gotten any easier. We still go through the same old routine.

"Each night about seven, when dinner is finished and he's enjoyed a half hour of television, we sit down together at the dining-room table and go over his assignments. I read the directions and sometimes I do the first problem with him to make sure he understands how to do it. He just sits there!

"So I begin to prod. 'Come on, get going!' I say. 'Let's get it done tonight before eight for a change.' He may do a problem or two, but then he just sits there again. So I prod some more, and he does a few more. This is how it goes for the first hour until bath time. If we're lucky, he may be half done.

"After the bath, it's more of the same. Sometimes, I get so frustrated I start yelling. This usually brings my husband in, and he has even less patience than I do. He starts yelling, too. Then Darren gets upset. So I console him, and my husband blames me for being too soft. It's crazy! I usually end up lecturing both of them, while Darren sneaks off to watch TV. Most nights, the homework doesn't get done.

"His teacher tells us Darren's homework should take about thirty to forty minutes. In our house it can drag on for hours! He won't do it unless we stand over him and make him do it."

And so it goes, Monday through Thursday, week after week, with his parents devoting a good portion of their evening pushing and prodding, threatening and lecturing, as Darren dawdles, avoids, and works as slowly as possible. Does homework really deserve this much attention? Is the act of getting it done really what's most important?

What Is the Purpose of Homework?

Sometimes, parents become so caught up in the task of getting it done that they lose sight of what homework is all about. Let's take a moment to consider why children are asked to do homework in the first place.

Homework teaches children two sets of lessons—one that is immediately apparent and one that requires us to look a little deeper. The most obvious reason for assigning homework is to provide children with opportunities to practice and improve their skills. Practice is essential to skill mastery. A regular homework routine helps children sharpen their skills. This is what Darren's parents were most concerned about. Let's call this Lesson #1.

But homework also teaches other, more important, lessons that can't be measured with letter grades—

responsibility, self-discipline, independence, perseverance, and time management. Homework teaches children how to begin a task on their own, stay with the task, complete it, and be responsible for the outcome. In the long run, these skills will have a much greater influence on a child's future success, not only in the classroom, but on the job and in life. These lessons are what Darren's parents and teacher were overlooking. Let's call this Lesson #2.

How do children learn this second set of lessons? By being allowed opportunities to stand on their own and do their part without interference from parents and teachers. The act alone conveys a powerful set of behavioral messages: "I believe you're capable." "I trust you to do this on your own."

A System out of Balance

When we look at all the steps the school and Darren's parents had taken to get Darren to do his homework, one question looms prominently: Whose homework is it, really? Darren's. But who keeps track of his assignments? Mom and the teacher. And who does part of the work? Mom and Dad. And who makes sure it gets turned in on time? Mom. And who experiences the consequences for the homework not getting done? Mom, Dad, and the school. If the homework really belongs to Darren, why, then, is everyone else doing his job for him?

What Darren's parents and teacher didn't realize is that they all had been playing hot potato with responsibility. And guess who ended up holding the potato? Not Darren. The way things were, he had little incentive for changing his behavior. He knew, from experience, that he could count on his teacher and parents to do his part for him.

Darren's parents and the school had fallen into a trap. They had been compensating for Darren's lack of responsibility by doing many of his jobs themselves. The more they compensated, the less Darren did, and the more out of balance their homework system became. Without realizing it, they were actually enabling him to behave the way he was, and he was getting a lot of negative attention in the process.

Sure, all their dancing was getting a little homework done, but at whose initiative? And what about Lesson #2? Things were not going to improve until they all got back to doing their rightful jobs.

"I think it's time we take a closer look at your homework system," I suggested to Darren's parents.

"Homework system?" said Darren's father, looking a little puzzled. "I don't think we have one, at least not one I'm aware of."

His response was not unusual. Most parents who become stuck in homework dances are not aware of the roles they play or that they operate within a system.

"Almost every parent has one," I said. "Yours just hasn't been working very well for you." I handed each of them a diagram like the one on the facing page (Figure 13A) and gave them a few minutes to look it over.

"Look familiar?" I asked. Both parents nodded. "This is what a homework system looks like when parents and teachers end up doing their children's jobs. We reviewed each list.

"How do things get this way?" Darren's father asked.

Some families just start off this way, that is, with their system out of balance. The jobs are not clear from the beginning or there's too much parent involvement. Parents think they are helping, but as time passes and patterns become established, they begin to notice that they do more and more while their children do less and less.

Other parents become overinvolved when the work is difficult and their children begin to struggle. The parents want to help, and they should up to a point, but when the

Figure 13A. Homework system out of balance

Parents' Jobs	Child's Jobs	Teacher's Jobs
Make frequent inquiries about assignments.	Provide excuses about assignments (such as, "It was lost, stolen; none was assigned; dog ate it").	Lecture, persuade, or coerce child to do the work.
Remind child to do his or her lessons.	Listen to reminders, lectures, reprimands from parents and teachers.	Give frequent reminders to do the lessons.
Ask if the work is done.	Wait until the last moment to get started.	Provide deadline extensions and extra-credit and makeup opportunities.
Make extra trips to school to pick up books or assignments.	Do the work in a busy place where it attracts maximum attention.	Make the work easier in hopes more will get done.
Help out by doing some of the work.	Pretend not to understand so parents will get involved.	Ask parents to become more involved.
Lecture or punish for not doing the work.	Rush through or do it carelessly to get it over with.	Provide special rewards for completed work.
Feel responsible for child's failures.	Blame parents and teacher for poor grades.	Feel responsible for child's failures.

helping is over and the child knows what to do, it's time to back off and let the child complete the task on his or her own. When parents fail to back off, the rescuing and over-involvement results in a gradual shifting of jobs.

The problem is gradual and insidious. In many cases, it may go unnoticed entirely until children stop doing their homework altogether like in Darren's home. By the time parents realize something is wrong, patterns have already become established, and a great deal of compensating has been going on.

Darren's mother looked confused. "Wait a second!" she said, pointing to the list of Parents' Jobs. "I thought I was supposed to do all these things. Are you saying that I shouldn't help Darren keep track of his assignments each day or remind him to turn in his homework?"

"Exactly right," I replied. "Not if you want to put your system back in balance and help Darren learn responsibility. That's not likely to happen until you stop doing Darren's jobs for him and limit your involvement to the jobs that are rightfully yours. What incentive will he have to do the work himself if he can always count on someone else to step in and bail him out?"

"But I know my son," she countered. "If I don't do those jobs, he won't, either."

"I think you're right," I agreed. "He probably won't until you build some consequences into your homework system to hold him accountable. As it is now, all Darren has to do is endure the prodding and lectures, and he's home free."

I could appreciate her confusion. Darren's mom was getting mixed messages about her appropriate level of involvement. Darren's teachers had asked her to become more involved with Darren's homework, but they gave her no specific plan for going about it. Like most parents, she interpreted the request to mean that she should do more of what she was already doing—more dancing. Now I was encouraging her to back off.

"How do we get off this treadmill?" asked Darren's father.

"You're right," I said. "It's time we started talking about how to hand the hot potato back to Darren and how to put your homework system in balance."

Putting the System Back in Balance

I handed Darren's parents a second diagram like the one on the following page (Figure 13B). "This is what the homework system looks like when it's in balance," I said. "Notice the distribution of responsibility between the three participants." I gave them a few minutes to look it over, then we reviewed each list of jobs.

In a balanced system, parents limit their involvement and operate as facilitators, they support and promote the homework process but play only a brief role. The key word here is "brief." Parents set limits on the jobs to be done, and they make sure children have everything they need to carry out their tasks, but that's where their job ends. The rest is up to the child. The child is the one who does the work.

"According to the chart, we should establish a regular time and a regular place for homework," said Darren's mother. "How is that different from what we've been doing?"

"Let's look at some guidelines for establishing times and places for homework in a balanced system," I suggested.

A Time for Homework

When helping parents select a suitable time for homework, keep three considerations in mind. First, they should select a time that can be used regularly. Homework should be a habit, a routine, something the child does on a regular basis.

Figure 13B. Homework system in balance

Parents' Jobs	Child's Jobs	Teacher's Jobs
Establish a regular time for homework.	Keep track of books and assignments.	Provide instruction.
Establish a regular place for homework.	Start on time and allow time to finish work.	Provide materials.
Provide necessary materials and supplies.	Do his or her own work with only limited assistance.	Provide deadlines.
Provide limited instruction and assistance.	Turn the work in on time.	Provide encouragement.
Establish logical consequences for non-compliance and follow through.	Accept responsibility for grades or other consequences.	Provide feedback regarding work returned.

When parents select a stable time, they help their child develop good work habits.

Second, parents should choose a time that is earlier rather than later. Why? Because children are generally fresher and more alert in the late afternoon or early evening than they are later on. They are more motivated to complete their jobs so they can get on to the "good stuff" that awaits them.

Also, there is an accountability issue to consider. When homework is the last task of the day before bed, what consequences are available to use if the child chooses not to comply? None. There's no accountability. The system breaks down. Late homework schedules eliminate opportunities to teach Lesson #2 with logical consequences. There is more than a little wisdom to the old axiom Work before play.

Finally, homework sessions should have a beginning and an end. That is, parents should specify the times they will be available to help and times when they are not. For example, if you expect your child to complete his or her homework between four-thirty and five, you might say, "I will be available to help between four-thirty and five, but not after that time." This is one of the surest ways to keep the hot potato in the child's lap and to define how much time parents are willing to devote to homework.

Time limits have other advantages, too. They teach children to plan and manage their time wisely, and they provide parents and children with time to enjoy each other's company without the intrusion of homework.

Sure, parents can be flexible and extend these deadlines for big exams and special projects, but otherwise, they should specify a regular homework period and do their best to stick to it. If they don't, they may be setting themselves up for long homework sessions or for providing opportunities for children to use homework as a device for garnering negative attention, power, and control over other family members. Again, homework is not worth this much attention.

How much time should parents set aside each day for homework? The guidelines I generally hear from teachers are thirty to forty-five minutes a night for primary-level children (grades one and two); thirty to sixty minutes a night for intermediate levels (grades three through six): and sixty to ninety minutes a night for secondary levels (grades seven through twelve). I recommend that parents consult with their child's teacher before deciding.

What if the child finishes in less than the allotted time? Terrific! If a brief review of the work reveals that it was, in fact, completed and a good effort was made to do it accurately, then there is no point in making him or her stay there to the end of the session. Even if some of the items are wrong? Yes, unless the child specifically asks his or her parents to check the work for accuracy. The emphasis should be on effort not outcome, process not product. If the child puts forth a good effort and does the work, that's enough. It doesn't have to be perfect to fulfill Lessons #1 and #2.

A Place for Homework

Where should homework be done? The best place for homework is a separate, quiet area away from parents and other family members. A balanced system is difficult to maintain when parents allow children to do homework at the kitchen table or in other busy family areas. Parents risk that homework will receive more attention and parental involvement than it deserves. That's an invitation to dance.

If not the kitchen or dining room, then where? A child's bedroom, a study, or another quiet room works fine for homework provided they are available on a regular basis, away from traffic and distractions such as TV or other family activities, and provisioned with all the right equipment and materials such as a desk, comfortable chair, lamp, supply of paper, pencils, pens, a dictionary, ruler, tape, paper clips, and maybe a tray or two to keep things organized.

"How do we get this new system going?" asked Darren's mother, relieved at the prospect that help was on the horizon.

Three Steps to a Balanced System

The good news for any parent who wants to end the dance and pass the hot potato back to their child is that the remedy requires less time, energy, and involvement than they are already putting forth. The three steps they will need to follow include clarifying the jobs, building in accountability, and staying off the dance floor.

Step 1: Clarify the Jobs

When I assist parents in repairing a broken system, I always recommend that they sit down with their child and explain the various jobs in a balanced system—the parents' jobs, the teacher's jobs, and the child's jobs. I encourage parents to be very specific about how, when, and where the child should carry out his or her jobs. Some parents find it helpful to post the jobs and time schedules on the refrigerator to eliminate confusion. This is what I encouraged Darren's parents to do.

"OK," said Darren's father, "the system sounds good in theory, but what happens when Darren chooses not to do his jobs?"

"This is where your accountability measures come in," I replied. In a balanced system, children are accountable for their poor choices because they experience regular and consistent consequences when they choose not to do their part. Consequences provide motivation for making good choices.

Step 2: Build Accountability into the System

When children find a way to avoid homework on a regular basis, often it's because their homework system lacks accountability. They are not likely to change their behavior until their parents build some accountability into the system. How do parents do this? First, they need a procedure for monitoring their child's assignments to make sure the assigned work actually gets home. Second, they need to follow through with logical consequences when their child chooses to do less than his or her part.

Let's begin with procedures for monitoring assignments. There are many creative ways to monitor assignments, but I prefer two methods in particular because they are brief, simple, and require little parental involvement. The monitoring system for elementary students consists of one assignment sheet for the entire week that goes home with the child on Mondays (Figure 13C). The teacher writes down the assignments and indicates any outstanding assignments in the space at the bottom of the sheet. It's the child's responsibility to get the assignment sheet home. Consequences, such as loss or reduction of that day's privileges, go into effect if that doesn't happen.

The monitoring procedure for secondary students is more complicated because more teachers are involved. Each day, it's the student's responsibility to write down his or her assignments on a daily assignment sheet and present the sheet to the teacher. The teacher checks it for accuracy, initials it, and notes any outstanding assignments or incomplete work at the bottom of the form (Figure 13D). It's the student's job to bring the sheet home.

If the student fails to bring his or her initialed assignment sheet home, then consequences should go into effect that afternoon. If the student does bring the initialed sheet home and does the work during the time required, then parents simply compare work assigned to work completed and allocate privileges.

Does monitoring take away some of the child's responsibility? Yes, it does, a little, but very little in comparison to the amount of responsibility it keeps on the child for doing the rest of his or her jobs. Monitoring simply removes the gray area about what jobs need to be done and provides parents with a basis for evaluating if assigned work has been completed.

**Figure 13C. Sample assignment
sheet for elementary students**

**HOMEWORK FOR WEEK
February 24–28**

MONDAY

Read Chapter One in *Explorers* (pages 10–22).
Answer five study questions at end of chapter.

TUESDAY

Review spelling list.
Write each word in a complete sentence.
Bring materials for science experiment: jar with lid, candle.

WEDNESDAY

Complete 25 division problems on page 119 in math book.
Answer five work problems on page 120.

THURSDAY

Read Chapter Two in *Explorers* (pages 23–31).
Answer five study questions at end of chapter.
Study map on page 24 for quiz on Friday.

Figure 13D. Sample assignment sheet for secondary students

Date _____

Class: _____   **Assignment due:** _____

Assignment:

                                  Teacher's initials:_____

Class: _____   **Assignment due:** _____

Assignment:

                                  Teacher's initials:_____

Class: _____   **Assignment due:** _____

Assignment:

                                  Teacher's initials:_____

Class: _____   **Assignment due:** _____

Assignment:

                                  Teacher's initials:_____

Class: _____   **Assignment due:** _____

Assignment:

                                  Teacher's initials:_____

Now, let's look at the second part of the accountability system—consequences. When applied consistently, logical consequences help children learn responsibility and Lesson #2 by holding them accountable for their choices. All parents need to do is follow through and enforce the consequence without dancing. No lectures. No threats. No reminders or angry displays. When children hold the hot potato, they learn from their own mistakes.

What is a logical consequence for not doing homework? If homework is the child's job and after-school privileges are the paycheck for a job completed, then temporary loss of after-school privileges is an effective logical consequence.

The system is really very simple. Privileges are based on performance. If the child brings home all of his or her assignments and completes all assigned work during the designated time, then he or she receives full after-school privileges for that day. If the child completes all of his or her homework assignments for the entire week, then he or she earns full weekend privileges.

If, on the other hand, the child fails to bring home his or her assignments or fails to complete his or her work within the agreed-upon time, then parents should follow through and withhold some or all of that child's after-school privileges. Call it "a quiet time in the house" and take it one day at a time. Incomplete work should be completed during a designated time on Saturday or Sunday, but not both. In short, each school day the child earns privileges not only for that day but for the weekend as well.

Consequences for Elementary School Students

No after-school play privileges

No visiting with friends

No TV or video games

Spend time in the house doing quiet activities

Consequences for Secondary Students

No after-school free-time privileges

No visiting with friends

No telephone privileges

No TV or video game privileges

Spend quiet time in the house doing quiet activities

Revised limits on curfew, dating, car use, or telephone privileges based on level of compliance

Step 3: Stay off the Dance Floor

After parents clarify the jobs to be done and put their accountability measures in place, they are ready to back off and let their homework system teach its lessons. The hot potato is now in the child's lap, and parents should see that it stays there. How do they do that? By limiting their involvement to their own jobs and by enforcing their accountability system.

"How long will it take to get things back in balance once we put this new system into effect?" asked Darren's father.

What You Should Expect

Every parent wants to hear the good news that things will get better quickly. But some problems, such as homework dances, don't lend themselves to a quick fix. Changing old habits takes time. I had confidence Darren's parents would be successful because they were motivated to do what was needed, but I wanted to be sure that they left my office with a realistic set of expectations. I tried to put things in perspective.

"Your homework dances have been going on for quite a while," I observed. "Things will probably get worse before they get better. That is, Darren will need to experience repeatedly the consequences associated with his poor choices before he is likely to change his behavior. This takes time, perhaps three to six weeks or more. When it does happen, and it should, you will also begin to see a lot more of Lesson #1."

During the transition period, parents should expect testing. Their children will probably continue to make excuses about lost or forgotten assignments, dawdle, procrastinate, or put on displays of confusion or helplessness. They may even intensify their routines in a desperate attempt to get Mom and Dad to rescue, lecture, punish, or do more than just their rightful part.

As tempting as the bait may be, encourage parents to keep their limits firm and follow through with the three-step plan. The testing won't last forever. It's just a normal, but stressful, part of the change process.

As suggested, Darren's parents reviewed their new homework system with Darren and put it into effect the next day. They established a four o'clock start time with an upper limit of five o'clock. Neither parent would be available to help after five o'clock unless arrangements were made in advance. The schedule allowed Darren plenty of time to have a snack after school and time to play with friends or watch TV if he finished his work promptly.

Darren's father set up a desk in Darren's room upstairs and provisioned it with all the necessary stuff. If Darren needed help, it was his job to go downstairs and ask for it, then return to his room to do the work.

For accountability, Darren's parents and teacher decided to use the weekly assignment sheet and the monitoring system I recommended. They informed Darren that it was his responsibility to bring the sheet home on Monday. If that didn't happen, his after-school play privileges were suspended each day until it did. No excuses were accepted.

If Darren completed all his jobs each day and did his own work within the allotted time, he received full privileges for that day. He could visit with friends, go outside and play, watch TV, and enjoy his evening without restrictions.

If Darren chose not to do his jobs, he lost his privileges for that day and spent the hour before dinner from five until six in his room. After dinner, he spent a quiet time in the house without TV or video games. On Saturdays between nine and one, he was expected to finish all of his incomplete work for the week before he could play with his friends.

Two weeks after our first session, Darren's parents returned for a follow-up visit. "How did it go?" I asked.

"Well, we didn't see much homework completed until very recently," said Darren's father, "but we didn't hear much fighting, either."

"He's right," agreed Darren's mother. "For the first time in months, my stomach hasn't been in knots before dinner. Our home has been a much more peaceful place to live."

"Did Darren do much testing?" I inquired.

"As predicted," said his mother. "He didn't bring his assignment sheet home until Wednesday of the first week, but we followed through with consequences—no play privileges. When he finally did bring it home, he informed us that he wasn't going to do it. 'That's up to you,' I said. When four o'clock rolled around each day, I made sure he was in his room. Then I announced that I would be available until five to help but not afterward. He never asked. In fact, he didn't do any homework that first week," she continued. "He just sat there. So, we followed through— no play privileges. He spent the hour before dinner in his room, and after dinner, it was quiet time. On Saturday, he made no efforts to do the work, so he was restricted to the house. When his friends came by, we informed them that he couldn't play."

"How did he handle all that?" I inquired.

"At first he said he didn't care," said Darren's father, "but later he cried and told us we were mean and unfair. This past week, he's been scowling and glaring at us a lot in the evenings."

"You mentioned that he did complete some work toward the end of the two-week period?" I inquired.

"Yes, on Thursday, he just went up to his room and did it!" said his mother. "I thought he was pouting, so you can imagine my surprise at five o'clock when he handed over his completed work and headed out to play. The strange thing was, it was no big deal to him. That evening, we all watched a program together, and he acted like nothing happened.

"On Saturday, he surprised us again. He had accumulated a fair amount of leftover homework during the week. We anticipated another day of moping and scowling and turning friends away at the door. But after breakfast, Darren headed up to his room and finished all of his work by ten-thirty. Three days' worth! Then, off he went. No big deal."

Their homework system was working. For two weeks, Darren held the hot potato by himself with no one to pass it to. He tried avoidance, then defiance, then waited for the rescue that never came. Lesson #2 was beginning to sink in, and Lesson #1 wasn't far behind.

Darren and his parents were well on their way to a successful outcome. They just needed more time for their system to teach its lessons. I agreed to meet with them every two weeks and follow their progress.

The improvement continued. By the end of week four, Darren completed more homework than he left unfinished and did the mop-up work quickly on Saturdays. The pattern continued into week six. His grades were improving. On week eight, all homework assignments were completed on time. A milestone! Saturday wasn't needed.

By week ten, Darren was showing initiative and independence by heading off to his room before the usual prompt of "Time for homework." His parents decided to reduce their monitoring to random spot-checks of completed work. Darren was so eager to get out to play each day that he didn't even notice. By week twelve, Darren showed full compliance. Their system was in balance.

When they came in for their final follow-up session, Darren's parents were pleased, and with good reason. The homework battles that dominated their house had been gone for many weeks. Darren was doing his part independently, and his grades showed it. Things seemed to be fixed. But were they really?

Change can be fragile, particularly during the early stages of implementing a homework system. Lapses sometimes occur, and they can happen to parents just as easily as children. It begins with a missed assignment here and a reminder there, more missed assignments, more reminders, maybe a lecture or two, and before they know it, parents are dancing again!

Keeping a system in balance requires vigilance on the parents' part. I encouraged Darren's parents to be on guard for lapses and relapses and to be prepared to increase their monitoring procedures if Darren slipped back into old patterns. They had worked hard to put things back in balance. I wanted them to leave with the tools to see that things stayed that way.

When Professional Help Is Needed

In Darren's case, the three-step system was an effective remedy because homework really was the primary problem and not just a symptom of something larger going on. But this is not always easy to determine. If parents do not see significant improvement during the first six weeks, then they may need assistance from a qualified professional.

If you recall, I began my work with Darren and his parents by conducting an evaluation. A number of factors were considered: possible learning problems; behavioral problems; emotional issues; family, communication, and relationship problems. With teens, I routinely investigate possible problems with depression, drugs, or alcohol. After reviewing Darren's background information, I felt comfortable that homework was the primary concern.

You may need to recommend the same type of evaluation when parents do not encounter anticipated progress during the first six weeks. Encourage them to make an appointment with a licensed psychologist, educational psychologist, or other qualified helping professional.

Questions and Answers

1. *How do parents get children started with good homework habits?*

Answer: The best way is to begin with a homework system in balance. That is, parents and children should do their own jobs, and only their jobs, at regular times and in regular places.

2. *When should parents implement the three-step homework system?*

Answer: If a child avoids his or her homework responsibilities on a regular basis, then it's time to implement the three-step system.

3. *When parents inform me that their children do homework late in the evening at the dining-room table, should I encourage them to change this practice?*

Answer: As you know, I don't recommend late homework schedules or allowing children to do homework in busy family areas, but these habits do not always lead to problems. If Lessons #1 and #2 are taking place, then I don't recommend tampering with their system.

4. *Do younger children need more help getting started with their homework?*

Answer: Yes, and this is a major reason why many parents get overinvolved early on. Younger children usually do require more prompts to get started and more assistance with directions. If parents keep their prompts and assistance to a minimum, then they will be sending the right messages.

5. *What can teachers do in the classroom to hold students accountable for completing their homework?*

Answer: At the elementary-school level, classroom teachers can encourage good homework habits with a clever accountability procedure called Fun Friday. Fun Friday is a preferred activity period, held on Friday afternoons. Students become eligible for Fun Friday when they have completed all of their homework assignments for the week. Those who are not eligible use the time to catch up on their unfinished homework. In effect, Fun Friday becomes an incentive for compliance and an instructive logical consequence for noncompliance. Although the procedure supports parents' efforts, it is not a suitable substitute for an effective accountability system in the home.

6. *Should I ask the parents of all of my students to initial completed homework assignments to help them become more aware of their child's compliance with homework?*

Answer: The gesture is well-intentioned, but probably not very helpful. The practice may even send the wrong message to your compliant students by encouraging parent overinvolvement.

7. *If parents implement the three-step system with good results, how long should they wait before they discontinue monitoring?*

Answer: I recommend that parents taper off gradually rather than drop their monitoring all at once. After four to six weeks of full compliance, parents should conduct random spot-checks for another eight to twelve weeks. If full compliance continues, then they are probably ready to discontinue monitoring altogether. They should be ready to reinstate the procedure if needed.

8. *Do lapses on the child's part indicate that the system doesn't work?*

Answer: No. Lapses indicate that the child still has more learning to do. Lesson #2 is not complete. It's time to resume the three-step system.

9. *What should parents do when they check their child's work for compliance and discover that most of it was done hurriedly and carelessly?*

Answer: This is probably limit testing or the child's attempt to determine the parent's minimum standards for acceptable work. If the child's work doesn't satisfy the parent's definition of a good effort, then the parent should be clear about what is expected and ask the child to go back and finish up.

10. *Do you recommend that parents give prizes or special rewards when children complete their homework on time?*

Answer: No. This sends the wrong message. Usually special rewards are reserved for special accomplishments. The parent is not asking that they do anything special. Positive acknowledgment and the usual privileges should be enough.

Chapter Summary

Homework takes place in a system involving three participants: the parents, the teacher, and the child. Each has their own set of jobs to carry out if the system is to operate smoothly and remain in balance. The system can break down, and often does, when its members do less than or more than their own part. Teachers are in an ideal position to help parents put their system back in balance.

The key to a balanced homework system is helping parents do their part, and only their part, without taking responsibility away from the child or the teacher. Parents should establish a regular time for homework, a regular place for homework, and logical consequences for noncompliance. Once the system is set up, all parents need to do is follow through and let the system teach the lessons it was intended to teach. Homework can, and should be, a lesson in responsibility, independence, perseverance, and time management.

▼

Chapter
14

Helping Students with Hyperactivity and Inattention

Corey, age five, is in constant motion. He always seems to be out of his seat. Colin, age seven, blurts out comments or answers whenever he feels like it. He becomes upset when corrected. Mikala, age eleven, is easily distracted. She requires frequent refocusing to stay on task. Brent, age fourteen, has been suspended nine times for disruption. He seldom completes his work and is failing many of his classes.

What do all of these students share in common? All sit in regular classrooms with twenty-five or more students, and all have, or are suspected of having, a condition called ADD, or Attention Deficit Disorder. Students with ADD pose some of the most challenging behavior management problems teachers confront in the classroom. They require a lot of structure, support, and consistent guidance to keep them on track and to help them perform to the best of their ability.

This chapter will help you understand the special needs of students with ADD and learn the behavior management tools you'll need to work with them effectively. We will begin by reviewing some basic information about the disorder: what it is, how it's diagnosed, and how it's treated. Then we will follow four cases from referral to intervention so you can see how to develop an effective treatment plan. By the time you're done, you'll know how to recognize the symptoms of ADD and how to provide the structure and behavior management ADD students need to be successful. Teachers are the key to successful intervention.

What Is Attention Deficit Disorder?

Imagine that you're nine years old. You're sitting in class. Your teacher just gave directions for the next assignment, but you missed most of what she said because you were playing with the bead chain of the zipper on your jacket. You look around to figure out what to do and notice that others have their science books out. So you pull yours out, too, but you still don't know what to do. When you ask the boy sitting next to you, he gives you a dirty look and tells you to stop bothering him. You ask someone else; she does the same thing then tells you to ask the teacher.

"Mrs. Peters," you blurt out, "I don't know what to do." Oops! You disturbed the class. She looks annoyed.

"What are you supposed to do when you need my help?" your teacher asks.

You remember and raise your hand, and she comes over to help. She repeats her original instructions, then prods you a little to get you started. "You only have ten minutes," she says. "If you don't finish on time, you'll have to take it home as homework."

Finally you're focused. You complete the first two items then become distracted when you hear someone using the pencil sharpener. You look around the room for a while, then refocus and do a few more items. Halfway through the assignment, your teacher announces that it's time to put everything away and get ready for recess. You clear your desk and wait quietly. It pays off. Your teacher excuses your group first, but as soon as she does, you sprint for the door to be first in line. She calls you back.

"We don't run in the classroom," she says. "You need to wait until everyone else has been excused, then go to the back of the line." Reluctantly you return to your seat.

Can you imagine what school would be like if this was how you spent most of your days? How do you think you would feel toward your classmates who avoided you? Or toward your teacher who constantly corrected you? Most important, how do you think you would feel about yourself? This is only the tip of the iceberg for many children with ADD. The problems they face at school usually mirror similar problems at home.

ADD is a term commonly used to describe a syndrome known in the clinical literature as Attention Deficit Hyperactivity Disorder or ADHD. The syndrome has both neurological and behavioral features and is characterized by impairment in three specific areas: attention span, impulse control, and activity level. Although most children with the disorder exhibit the combined symptoms of inattentiveness, impulsivity, and hyperactivity, some show a preponderance of symptoms in one specific area. Hyperactivity is not essential for the diagnosis.

ADD is a fairly common childhood disorder. Conservative estimates indicate that ADD affects 3 to 5 percent of the school-age population with a greater prevalence of boys than girls. The disorder is represented among all racial, cultural, and socioeconomic groups.

Contrary to earlier beliefs, most children do not outgrow their symptoms when they reach adolescence. Recent research shows that ADD is a chronic disorder with symptoms first appearing during the preschool years and extending, in most cases, into adolescence. According to information released by C.H.A.D.D., a national organization for children and adults with attention deficit disorders, 30 to 70 percent show symptoms into adulthood. Most children with the disorder are not diagnosed until they reach elementary school and experience significant school performance problems.

What symptoms are you most likely to observe at school? Symptoms of inattention include: a high degree of distractibility, difficulty listening and following directions, difficulty focusing and staying on task, difficulty keeping track of books and assignments, and a tendency to bounce from one uncompleted task to another. Children who show symptoms of inattention without hyperactivity are often the most difficult to diagnose. They are frequently described as "spacey" and overlooked for ADD.

Symptoms of hyperactivity vary with age and developmental level. For example, preschoolers are more likely to show excessive gross-motor activity—more running, climbing, and general roughhousing than their peers. Elementary and secondary students, on the other hand, are more likely to display excessive restlessness and fidgeting in class. Symptoms of impulsivity are similar across age groups. They include difficulty staying seated and taking turns, blurting out comments and answers, excessive talking, interrupting, and a tendency to engage in dangerous playground activities.

In addition to the three groupings of symptoms, ADD students often display a number of secondary characteristics such as poor fine-motor coordination and handwriting problems, tantrums and temper outbursts, and a tendency to become oppositional and defiant when corrected. Because they have difficulty following directions and rules, their behavior brings them into more frequent conflict with their teachers and peers. By necessity, ADD children require a lot of corrective feedback.

Many ADD students are easily frustrated and overwhelmed by the quantity or difficulty of the work they encounter. To reduce their frustration, they try avoiding their work, which sets a self-defeating pattern in motion. The more they avoid, the further behind they become and the more frustration and discouragement they experience. Without intervention, many become stuck in a vicious cycle of frustration and avoidance and end up falling behind in their schoolwork.

You can probably think of many students who have shown some of these symptoms from time to time. Does this mean they have ADD? Not necessarily. At times, nearly all children show some of the behaviors I've described. This is normal. But children with ADD show more of these behaviors more often. Most importantly, the behaviors they display have an impairing affect on their achievement, class conduct, peer relationships, and general school performance. Level of impairment is the critical issue.

Do students with ADD show their symptoms all the time? No, and the variability in performance creates a confusing picture. ADD children have their on days when they are more focused and controlled and their off days when they are less focused and poorly controlled, but they have many more off days than their classmates. The pattern of behavior over time is a distinguishing feature of the disorder.

The good news is that ADD is treatable. In most cases, symptoms can be managed and controlled, and children can be helped to achieve closer to their full potential. Teachers play a key role in the identification and treatment process. The earlier children are identified, the sooner they can be helped to overcome the impairing effects of this disorder.

Without early identification and treatment, however, children run a greater risk for a variety of problems—school failure, poor self-esteem, poor social adjustment, family problems, emotional and behavior problems, dropping out of school, delinquency, substance abuse, and other mental health problems.

If the profile of ADD symptoms describes some of your students, encourage their parents to make an appointment with a child psychologist or pediatrician. If your school provides assessment services through a multidisciplinary team, then refer the child for a school-based assessment. Often referral by a concerned teacher is the first and most important step in the identification process.

Evaluating Attention Deficit Disorders

How are students evaluated for ADD? There is no single medical or psychological test that provides a definitive diagnosis of ADD. Most clinicians rely on a variety of sources to collect their data—a thorough developmental and medical history; behavior rating scales completed by both the teacher and parents; a review of previous school records; observations of the child in the home and classroom; and interviews with the parents, teacher, child, and others.

When learning problems are reported or the child is performing below grade level, some clinicians, including myself, routinely administer a battery of intellectual, perceptual-motor, and academic tests to determine if learning disabilities contribute to the child's achievement problems. Approximately 30 percent of children with ADD also have learning disabilities.

Who should conduct the ADD assessment? In the past, evaluations were performed almost exclusively by physicians and psychologists. More recently, schools have become involved in the process in an attempt to comply with Section 504 of the Rehabilitation Act of 1973, which recognizes ADD as a disability and requires a school-based assessment. School-based assessment is generally carried out by a multidisciplinary team that collects data from many sources and follows diagnostic criteria specified in *The Diagnostic and Statistical Manual of the American Psychiatric Association (DSM IV)*.

To qualify for the diagnosis of ADD, a child must exhibit a sufficient number of symptoms specified in *DSM IV,* show onset of the disorder before age seven, demonstrate impairment in at least two settings (home and classroom), and symptoms must be present for at least six months. Also, the clinician must rule out other medical, emotional, or environmental factors, such as ineffective limit setting or earlier traumatic experiences, that might cause similar symptoms. The level of impairment the symptoms cause should be specified as mild, moderate, or severe. Each level has important implications for treatment.

Treatments for ADD

The most effective treatment for ADD is a multimodal approach that combines a number of therapies—medical management, classroom accommodations, behavior modification, and counseling. These therapies are typically carried out in a collaborative effort by a team consisting of the parents, teachers, educational specialists, physicians, and behavioral or mental health professionals.

Think of the complete treatment as a combination of external and internal controls plus support (Figure 14A). External controls are provided through increased

Figure 14A. Treatments for ADD

External controls
(Structure / Behavior modifications)
+
Internal controls
(Medications)
+
Support
(Counseling)
↓
Improved symptom management
Better performance

structure, classroom accommodations, and behavior modification. Internal controls are enhanced through medications, and support is provided through counseling. Once a child is identified with the disorder, the clinician must determine the appropriate combination of therapies needed for effective symptom management or relief.

Not all children with ADD require the full combination of therapies. Some with mild symptoms show significant improvement after external controls have been increased at home and in the classroom. Others, particularly those with moderate to severe symptoms, require the full combination of internal and external controls to achieve the desired outcome. The need for support varies from case to case. Now that you have a clearer picture of the overall approach to treatment, let's take a closer look at each of the treatment components.

Medical Management

A variety of medications have been used successfully in the treatment of ADD. The most widely used medication is Ritalin, a psychostimulant, which provides effective symptom relief in many children with minimal side effects.

Cylert and Dexedrine are other psychostimulants used in the treatment of ADD. A variety of antidepressant medications including Tofranil, Norpramine, and imipramine also have been shown to provide good symptom relief.

How do these medications work? All are believed to act upon the body's neurotransmitter chemicals to improve attention span and impulse control, the primary neurological features of the disorder. Medications do not cure the disorder, but they provide effective temporary relief of symptoms so the child has a better opportunity to respond to the external controls in his or her environment. Medication should always be used in combination with other therapies.

Are there side effects associated with these medications? Some children may show side effects including among others appetite loss, disrupted sleep patterns, and lethargy at home and in the classroom. In many cases, these side effects can be controlled through dosage adjustments or changes in medication. It is important for teachers to keep parents informed of any negative side effects they might observe so parents can discuss them with their physician.

Classroom Accommodations

Students with ADD require structure, clear signals, and consistent rules to navigate successfully through their day. A well-organized classroom with the necessary modifications in instruction helps them perform to the best of their capabilities. The following tips should be helpful.

Organizing the Classroom

- Arrange for the ADD student to be seated near the teacher's desk, preferably at the front of a row with his or her back to other students and distractions. Desk groupings often create problems.

- Position the ADD student away from distracting stimuli such as pencil sharpeners, heaters, air-conditioner vents, doors, or high-traffic areas.

- Select responsible students as "buddy helpers" to assist the ADD student with questions, directions, and transitions. Be sure to rotate the job to avoid burning out helpers.

- Prepare ADD students with warnings prior to transitions (for example, "It's time to put your books away and get ready to go to the library"). Develop a plan or procedure for handling challenging situations such as lining up to go outside, getting on the bus, heading out to recess, and school assemblies or field trips.

- Post classroom rules and a daily classroom schedule.

- Place a tray or basket in a visible area near the front door for students to hand in homework, permission slips, or Friday folders.

- Redirect excess energy by providing classroom jobs such as erasing the blackboard, passing out papers, taking items to the office, or collecting lunch tickets.

- Provide a "quiet area" in the classroom for all students to use.

Modifying Instruction ADD students require greater structure, clarity, and consistency in the way class directions and assignments are presented and carried out. The following tips should be helpful.

- When possible, present one instruction at a time and keep all instructions clear and concise.

- Present instructions in both oral and written form whenever possible and be willing to repeat them in a positive manner.

- Encourage ADD students to ask for clarification or help when they don't understand what to do. Many won't ask for help and begin their tasks with incomplete information.

- When ADD students appear tuned out or unaware of what they are supposed to do, use the check-in procedure you learned in chapter 6.

- Develop a secret signal to use as a refocusing device when the ADD student is distracted or off task. Traditional methods such as "Hands in lap; eyes on me," also can be effective.

- ADD students are easily overwhelmed by the quantity of work they encounter. Break assignments down into manageable pieces and proceed step-by-step, offering encouragement for effort enlisted and praise for work completed. It may be necessary to reduce the length of the assignment.

- Provide extra time for completing some assignments or tests, particularly those requiring written work. Timed tasks are often difficult for children with short attention spans.

- When written assignments are a problem, allow for different modes of production such as word processors, scribes, or oral presentation.

- Help ADD students develop organizational strategies for keeping track of assignments, books, and materials and managing time.

- Encourage parents to implement a structured homework routine such as the system we covered in chapter 13. A single weekly homework assignment sheet is always preferable to a daily assignment sheet system.

Behavior Modification

What kind of behavior management works best with ADD students? ADD students do not require different behavior management, they just require more of it. The methods we've covered thus far in the book will be effective, but you should expect to use consequences more frequently. Why? Because ADD students miss many of your verbal signals. They require more action signals to stay on course.

What methods should be avoided? Punitive or permissive methods do not provide the clarity or support ADD students need to be successful. These methods set up conflicts and power struggles.

My counseling work often involves developing behavioral treatment programs for ADD students. One of the first steps I take, after reviewing my treatment plan with the parents and teacher, is to set up parallel behavior management programs in the home and classroom and run those programs simultaneously for eight weeks. Although the specific parts of the behavior management program vary from child to child, most require the following program components:

- Clear verbal messages (chapter 5)
- Check-in procedure and cooldown technique (chapter 6)
- Positive motivational strategies (chapter 7)
- Role-modeling, try it again, and limited choices (chapter 8)
- Logical consequences (chapter 11)
- Two-stage time-out procedure (chapter 12)

The parallel programs serve a number of purposes. First, they provide parents and teachers with the tools they need to manage the child's behavior. Second, the parallel programs provide the ADD student with a clear and consistent set of signals in his or her two primary settings. Third, the programs accelerate learning and behavior change by increasing treatment effect. Finally, the parallel behavior management programs provide me with an opportunity to evaluate the impact of increased structure and environmental controls on the child's overall performance.

At the end of the eight-week period, I arrange a follow-up conference with the various people involved in implementing the treatment programs—the parents, teachers, administrator, and other educational specialists. We review the child's progress and discuss the need for further interventions. Many children show a marked improvement in their behavior in response to the increased structure.

Supportive Counseling

ADD can be stressful, not only to the child with the disorder, but also to those who attempt to manage the child's behavior. Parents and teachers often feel overwhelmed, frustrated, and worn down. They need a lot of support and understanding to remain positive and stay on course. Counseling can make a difficult job a little easier.

Children with ADD also require support and assistance with developing appropriate social skills such as self-control, stress management, and problem solving. The counselor's office provides a safe and accepting atmosphere for learning and practicing new behaviors. The treatment is enhanced when parents and teachers encourage and reinforce the same skills at home and in the classroom.

Four Case Studies

In the final section of this chapter we will follow four cases from the point of referral to the development of an effective treatment plan. In each case, the appropriate combination of treatments resulted in significant improvement in the child's school performance, but the process did not always go smoothly. Each case illustrates some of the typical problems you can expect to encounter during the identification and treatment process.

Corey: A Kindergartner with ADD

Corey had been dismissed from three different preschools before he turned four. His parents thought his aggressive and rambunctious behavior would improve with time, so they held him out of preschool until he turned five, then started him in kindergarten. He was referred during the first week of school.

When Corey arrived at my office with his parents, I understood the reason for the speedy referral. He was all over the place. He ignored the usual books and puzzles I provide for my younger clients and found other ways to keep himself busy. He yanked on my blinds, grabbed items off my shelf, flicked my light switch off and on, and dumped the contents of my wastebasket all over the floor to see if there was anything interesting.

His parents did their best to restrain him, but each time he wiggled free and got into something new. He was a handful. Finally, Corey's father took him outside so Corey's mother and I could get started with the formal parts of the evaluation. We completed the necessary forms, discussed Corey's health and developmental history, and arranged a classroom observation and teacher interview for later that week.

The evaluation was revealing. Corey showed the full symptom picture of ADHD with moderate to severe impairment. He was constantly on the move—roughhousing, bouncing from one uncompleted activity to another, resisting requests for cooperation, and throwing tantrums when he didn't get his way.

Although Corey's behavior was not caused by ineffective limit setting, his parents' methods were not helping. His mother was permissive. She did a lot of repeating, reminding, reasoning, and explaining and usually gave in when he threw a tantrum or pushed her to the limit.

Corey's father, on the other hand, compensated for his wife's permissiveness by being very strict. He did a lot of shaming, blaming, yelling, and spanking. I could understand why Corey did so much hitting.

In the classroom, Corey was fortunate to have such a skilled teacher. Her signals were clear, firm, and consistent. She was highly effective, but she was beginning to wear down because Corey required frequent correction. He had extreme difficulty staying in his seat, paying attention, and following through on tasks. Morning circle and transition periods were his most difficult times of the day.

Her biggest concern, however, was Corey's aggressiveness. He constantly had his hands on other children—pushing, poking, grabbing, shoving, and hitting. She feared for their safety. Parents were beginning to complain.

Once the evaluation was complete, Corey's parents, teacher, principal, resource teacher, and I met as a team to discuss the results and develop a comprehensive home/school treatment plan. The evidence was clear. Corey needed the full combination of therapies, but his parents were reluctant to start him on medication until all other steps had been taken to improve his behavior. The team agreed to implement the following plan and meet again in eight weeks to review his progress and discuss the need for further steps.

Corey's Home/School Behavior Management Program

- Clear verbal messages (chapter 5)
- Check-in procedure and cooldown technique (chapter 6)
- Positive motivational methods (chapter 7)
- Role-modeling, try it again, and limited choices (chapter 8)

- Logical consequences and time-out procedure (chapters 11 and 12)

Corey's Classroom Accommodations

- Arrange seating near the teacher's desk.
- Provide a three-foot space between Corey and the nearest child in his table group.
- Use a carpet strip to define Corey's space during morning circle and floor activities.
- Develop special procedures to handle transitions such as lining up for recess or walking to the play area.
- Redirect Corey's excessive energy with classroom jobs.
- Provide a designated "quiet area" for cooldowns and in-class time-outs.
- Establish eye contact and repeat classroom directions and instructions as needed.
- Develop a secret signal to cue Corey when he needs to stop a disruptive behavior or get back under control.

Corey responded well to treatment, particularly at home. His parents were delighted. For the first time, they were able to manage his extreme behavior, even his tantrums, with success. He was beginning to tune in to their words and use acceptable problem-solving skills to get what he wanted.

At school, the results were mixed. Corey was more manageable during morning circle and transition periods. The cooldowns and time-outs also helped him regain lost self-control. But the grabbing, poking, and hitting continued, and so did the complaints from other parents. Corey's teacher was beginning to feel resentful.

The principal was also concerned. School policy required a suspension consequence for each hitting incident, but six suspensions in four weeks had little impact on

Corey's hitting. The principal had two remaining options—separate Corey from his classmates during recess or reduce the length of his instructional day. When she presented the options to his parents, they realized things had gone too far. They called their pediatrician and started Corey on medication a few days later.

Corey's teacher noticed the change right away. He was more attentive, stayed in his seat longer, and had a much easier time keeping his hands off others. The hitting stopped altogether. His disruptions were less frequent. Medication helped Corey respond to the structure and guidance he received in the classroom. His teacher's job was easier.

At our eight-week follow-up conference, the team agreed that the combination of treatments was on target. Corey's behavior had improved markedly, and everyone was encouraged by his progress. He still required more guidance than his classmates, but his behavior was manageable. Corey was achieving closer to his potential.

Colin: A Disruptive Second Grader

If there is such a thing as a typical ADD referral in my clinical work, then Colin fits the profile. He didn't appear impulsive, but the behavior-rating scales his teacher and parent completed showed that he frequently interrupted, blurted out comments, and had difficulty waiting his turn. Often he was out of his seat. He didn't seem distractible or inattentive, yet he seldom followed directions or completed his assignments. Colin did many of the things ADD students do, but there was a willful quality to the way he did them. When I explored his history and the guidance methods his mother and teacher used, I began to understand why.

At home, Colin ran the show, and he had been running the show since he was three. His mother, a single parent, was extremely permissive. She used a lot of repeating, re-minding, warnings, and second chances. When Colin be-came defiant, she usually gave in to avoid the confrontation. Colin was accustomed to getting his own way. He probably expected things to go the same way at school.

In the classroom, Colin's teacher used methods simi-lar to those he encountered at home. She typically started off with a lot of repeating and reminding, then gave warn-ings and second chances, but that's where the similarities ended. If Colin tuned her out or continued testing, which he usually did, she wrote his name on the board. If he per-sisted, she wrote a check after his name. If he became de-fiant, she took away a recess, made him call his mother, or gave him a citation to take home. None of these conse-quences had much impact. His teacher was wearing down.

The more information I collected, the less Colin looked like a child with ADD. Sure, he showed many of the symp-toms, but his symptoms were mild, and his behavior was what you might expect of a strong-willed child trained with permissiveness. Colin behaved like many of the aggressive researchers I see in my office. He pushed hard as long as others were willing to bend. He wasn't finding the firm lim-its he needed to keep him on course.

When I shared my diagnostic impressions with Colin's teacher, she was surprised. She never suspected her meth-ods might be contributing to the problem. Colin's mother wasn't surprised. She knew her son was calling the shots at home and believed he was probably trying to do the same thing at school. She was right.

I introduced the parallel behavior management pro-grams, and Colin's teacher and mother were eager to get started, But first we had some clean-up work to do. We needed to eliminate all the steps that weren't working. No more repeating or reminding. No more warnings or sec-ond chances. No drama or yelling. No names on the black-board, calls to Mom, or citations. When that was behind us, we put the following program into effect and ran it for eight weeks at home and in the classroom.

Colin's Behavior Management Program

- Clear verbal signals (chapter 5)
- Check-in procedure and cut-off technique (chapter 6)
- Try it again and limited choices (chapter 7)
- Logical consequences (chapter 11)
- Time-out procedure (chapter 12)

The consistency between home and school produced the change we all expected. Colin tested less and cooperated more. Each week, there were fewer disruptions. By week eight, everyone was convinced that he was capable of controlling his behavior. Colin was beginning to shine. Increased structure and consistent behavior management made the difference.

Mikala: An ADD Student with Learning Disabilities

When Mikala's parents arrived at my office, they weren't looking for an evaluation. Their fifth-grade daughter had been diagnosed with ADD in the first grade, and she had been taking Ritalin twice a day ever since. Her parents were concerned because they weren't seeing the improvement they expected. Each year had been a struggle.

By the time Mikala reached the fifth grade, she was nearly two years behind in her schoolwork. She complained that her assignments were too difficult, and she spent more time avoiding her work than completing it. When avoidance didn't work, she acted out and disrupted class. She was constantly in trouble.

I explored the various components of her treatment program to see if we could find some answers for her lack of progress. I began with medication. Mikala's parents reported that she was taking 20 milligrams of Ritalin twice a day, which provided good symptom relief during school hours, but no relief in the late afternoon when she started homework. Homework was a nightmare. She probably needed a third dose in the late afternoon.

Were the classroom accommodations helping? I wondered. When I asked her parents this question, they looked puzzled because no steps had been taken to accommodate Mikala's special needs. She was treated like everyone else. No preferential seating. No modifications in assignment length or time for completion. No adjustments for completing written work. Directions were given once, orally, and questions were discouraged. Unfinished assignments were added to homework. Clearly, this treatment component needed improvement.

Next I explored the guidance methods used at home and in the classroom. Mikala's parents both used the mixed approach. They did a lot of reasoning, lecturing, and explaining. When that didn't work, and it rarely did, they became angry and removed her privileges for long periods of time.

Mikala's teacher took a punitive approach to classroom discipline. She used a lot of shaming, blaming, and humiliation tactics to keep Mikala on task. When Mikala disrupted, which she did almost daily, her teacher made her write an apology letter to the class, copy the classroom rules, and bring a negative behavior report home to her parents. This set the tone for the rest of her day.

I was beginning to understand some of the reasons for Mikala's lack of progress. Her treatment program was running on only one of four cylinders, and the one that worked needed a tune-up in the afternoons. Mikala required the full combination of therapies, and perhaps she needed more. Her lagging achievement still concerned me.

Her parents and teachers had assumed that Mikala's academic problems were due to ADD and poor work habits, not to learning problems. Was this an accurate assumption? Approximately 30 percent of children with ADD also show learning disabilities. Mikala had been complaining for years that the work was too difficult. Maybe it was.

I arranged an evaluation session with Mikala and administered a battery of psychological and educational tests. The results confirmed what Mikala had been telling us all along. Some of the work was too difficult. She showed a profile of specific learning disabilities and qualified for special help. Now we had all the information we needed to request a conference with her school support team and put the full treatment program in place.

Mikala's parents, teacher, principal, resource specialist, teacher, and I met at the school to review the test results and discuss ways to help Mikala become more successful. We agreed to discontinue all the steps that weren't working. No more shaming or humiliation tactics. No more apology letters, copying classroom rules, or negative behavior reports. Mikala needed support and to experience success. We implemented the following treatment plan and agreed to review her progress in eight weeks.

Medical Management

- Mikala's parents agreed to consult with their pediatrician regarding an afternoon dose of medication to help Mikala get through homework.

Classroom Accommodations

- Arrange seating at the front of a row, near the teacher's desk.
- Select a responsible classmate to be Mikala's "buddy helper" and assist with directions and questions.
- Present directions in both oral and written form.
- Use a secret signal to cue Mikala to the need to refocus when she is off task.

- Modify the length of assignments, particularly homework assignments, and provide extra time for completion.
- Provide alternative methods for completing written assignments such as using a word processor or giving oral reports.
- Provide homework assignments for the week on one sheet of paper to be passed out on Monday.
- Provide special assistance three times weekly in reading and written language through the resource specialist in the special education program.

Home/School Behavior Management Program

- Clear verbal messages (chapter 5)
- Check-in procedure (chapter 6)
- Commendations and encouragement (chapter 7)
- Try it again and limited choices (chapter 8)
- Logical consequences (chapter 11)
- Time-out procedure (chapter 12)

Supportive Counseling

- Mikala's parents arranged individual counseling sessions for their daughter through their health plan.

At the eight-week follow-up conference, Mikala's parents and teacher reported a noticeable change in her behavior. She completed more work and did so with less complaining and avoidance. She looked forward to her sessions with the resource specialist. As she experienced greater success, her acting out decreased. By week five, time-outs were seldom needed.

The other components were helping, too. The afternoon dose of medication took much of the battle out of homework, and the counseling provided welcomed support. Mikala was beginning to feel good about herself. The combined treatment components were working.

Brent: A Secondary Student with ADD

The transition from elementary school to junior high school can be challenging for any student, but it can be particularly challenging for a student with ADD. There are more teachers to adjust to, more assignments to keep track of, more rules, more homework, and more transitions during the day. Secondary teachers have so many students that it's difficult to follow through with classroom accommodations. Consistent behavior management is hard to achieve when six or more teachers are involved.

This is what Brent was struggling with when I first met him. In elementary school he didn't require many classroom accommodations. He was bright and capable, and his medication helped him focus and pay attention. He didn't complete much homework, but he always managed to get B and C grades with little effort. His periodic disruptions were not a problem. His teachers refocused him or used the time-out procedure when he persisted. He usually settled down and got himself under control.

When Brent began seventh grade, however, things were different. He was assigned more homework, and it counted for a larger portion of his grades. He could no longer get by with strong in-class performances. When Brent disrupted in junior high school, the guidance he received varied greatly from teacher to teacher. Some made him sit outside the classroom. Others made him write apology letters or sent notes home to his parents. Two of his teachers criticized and ridiculed Brent in front of his peers. When he responded with defiance, which he often did, they sent him to the vice principal who usually suspended him.

By the end of his first semester, Brent had been suspended nine times for defiance, and he was failing four of his seven classes. His vice principal was considering transferring him to another campus.

When Brent's parents asked what they could do to help turn their son around, the vice principal suggested they withhold all of his after-school privileges until he shaped up. So that's what they did. No more TV, video games, using the telephone, or hanging out with friends. After school, he was expected to spend his time doing homework or studying for tests. His parents agreed to restore his privileges at the end of the next grading period if his grades improved and the suspensions stopped. It didn't help. The problems continued.

"We're very frustrated," said Brent's mother. "We've tried everything the school suggested, but things seem to be getting worse, not better. I know Brent is frustrated, too. " He nodded in agreement.

I could understand their frustration. Their homework system wasn't working, and the school was treating Brent's ADD as a discipline problem. His mother was right: The punitive measures were actually making matters worse. Brent needed at least three of the four components of an effective treatment plan, but only one was in effect—medication. My goal was to help them with the remaining two.

I showed Brent and his parents how to set up a balanced homework system. From now on, it would be Brent's job to write down all of his assignments, bring all of his materials home, and do his work on time. No more nagging or badgering or drawn-out consequences. If he did his part, then he enjoyed full privileges for that day. If not, he spent the remainder of the day in the house without TV, video games, use of the telephone, or visits from friends. Brent liked the plan, but his mother anticipated a problem.

"What should we do if he comes home without his books or assignments and tells us he doesn't have any homework?" she asked. "We have no way of knowing."

I explained the daily assignment sheet system and the accountability procedure of having Brent's teachers initial his assignments for accuracy. If he shows up without the initialed assignment sheet, then consequences go into effect for that day.

His mother liked the idea. No more loopholes. Now, it was clear what he had to do. I thought his teachers would support the plan, too, as it required only a few seconds of their time. Their homework problem looked fixable. Next we needed to put a more effective behavior management system in place.

At home, Brent's parents used the time-out procedure with good success. If his junior-high-school teachers were willing to use the procedure, we would have better consistency between home and school. When I shared the plan with Brent, he said he preferred time-outs to writing apology letters or trips to the office.

Most teens like to have input in the decisions that affect them. Brent was no exception. When I asked him how he could prevent further suspensions, he was candid.

"Someone should tell my third- and sixth-period teachers to lighten up. I like to be asked, not ordered or put down."

He wanted to be asked respectfully, a reasonable request, but I didn't know if we could achieve it. I didn't know if his two teachers would be willing to change their approaches, but I did think they would be willing to use a secret signal to cue Brent when he was off task or disrupting. If I suggested the plan to all of his teachers, the two that needed it most would not feel singled out. Brent and his parents liked the plan. I called the school and arranged a conference with his various teachers, the vice principal, his guidance counselor, his parents, and of course, Brent and myself.

When I shared the ideas about initialing Brent's daily homework assignments and using a secret signal to alert Brent to his behavior, his teachers were happy to cooperate. They agreed to announce the time remaining in the period each time Brent was off task or disrupting. That was his cue to get back on task. Several wanted to use the plan with other students.

Next, I recommended that all of his teachers use the two-stage time-out procedure when Brent persisted in his disruptions. No more apology letters, notes home, or trips to the office. I explained how the procedure worked. Stage-one time-outs would take place in the classroom, and stage-two time-outs would take place in a buddy teacher's classroom. Brent's favorite teacher volunteered his classroom for all second-stage time-outs. The vice principal looked relieved to be out of the discipline loop.

The new treatment plan was brief and easy to carry out. All agreed to run it for eight weeks then meet again to evaluate Brent's progress. Brent's new treatment plan included the following.

Classroom Accommodations

- Teachers will initial Brent's daily homework assignment sheet for accuracy (chapter 13).

Behavior Management Plan

- Teachers will use a secret signal to cue Brent when he is off task or disrupting.
- Teachers will use a two-stage time-out procedure when Brent persists with his disruptions (chapter 12).

At the eight-week follow-up conference, everyone wore smiles, particularly Brent. His homework was coming in regularly, and his grades had improved to Bs and Cs. The secret signal helped him refocus and get back on task. He didn't disrupt any less than before, but now his teachers had the tools to manage his behavior more effectively. The time-out procedure worked. No more suspensions. Brent was back on track thanks to the combined treatments and the cooperative efforts of his parents and teachers.

Chapter Summary

In this chapter, we examined ADD, a fairly common and treatable childhood disorder that often impairs school performance. Children with ADD require a great deal of structure, support, consistent guidance, and in many cases, medication, to keep them on track and to help them perform to the best of their ability. Successful treatment often involves the combined efforts of teachers, parents, physicians, and helping professionals, but teachers play perhaps the most important role in the overall process. In each of the case examples we followed, the interventions teachers carried out in the classroom contributed most to the child's success. Teachers are the key to successful intervention.

▼

———————

Appendix

Suggestions for
Getting Started

I recommend starting off with the following skills for students of different ages. I've also included a suggested schedule for adding new skills as you move along. These suggestions are based on my experiences with teachers in my staff development workshops. You may prefer to add new skills to your repertoire at a faster or slower rate.

Whatever you choose, I encourage you to go at a pace that is comfortable for you. For some, this may mean adding one or two new skills each week , but for others it may mean adding one new skill every two or three weeks. There is no one correct way, but I caution you against trying to learn too much too quickly.

You should expect to make mistakes as you begin practicing the methods. That's OK. The more you practice, the more proficient you will become. If you are having particular difficulty with any one method, refer back to the pertinent chapter for assistance. Note the specific language used to set up and carry out each technique in the examples.

Getting Started with Preschool Students

Week 1
Clear verbal messages	Chapter Five
Check-in, cut-off, cooldown	Chapter Six
Encouraging messages	Chapter Seven
Logical consequences	Chapter Eleven
Two-stage time-out procedure	Chapter Twelve

Week 2
Add try it again	Chapter Eight
Add role-modeling	Chapter Eight

Week 3
Add limited choices	Chapter Eight

Week 4
Add natural consequences	Chapter Ten

Getting Started with Elementary School Students

Week 1
Clear verbal messages	Chapter Five
Check-in, cut-off, cooldown	Chapter Six
Encouraging messages	Chapter Seven
Logical consequences	Chapter Eleven
Two-stage time-out procedure	Chapter Twelve

Week 2
Add try it again	Chapter Eight
Add role modeling	Chapter Eight

Week 3
Add limited choices	Chapter Eight

Week 4
Add exploring choices	Chapter Eight

Getting Started with Secondary Students

Week 1

Clear verbal messages	Chapter Five
Check-in, cut-off, cooldown	Chapter Six
Encouraging messages	Chapter Seven
Logical consequences	Chapter Eleven

Week 2

Exploring choices	Chapter Eight
Two-stage time-out procedure	Chapter Twelve

Week 3

Add limited choices	Chapter Eight

Week 4

Add natural consequences	Chapter Ten

▼

Index

A

Abstract-thinking skills, 158
Acceptable actions, encouragement of, 137–138
Accountability procedures, 15–17
  Friday work folders, 16
  Fun Friday, 16
  for homework, 236–239
  makeup sessions for missed work, 16–17
  for OCS referral forms, 199
  for time-outs, 213–214
Action messages. *See also* Logical consequences
  discouraging action messages, 132–133
  firm limits, example of, 112
  firm message supported by, 111
ADD students, 249–275
  behavior modification for, 259–261
  case studies, 261–275
  classroom accommodations for, 257–259

  counseling for, 261
  defined, 250–254
  evaluation of, 254–255
  external controls for, 255–256
  extra time for students, 259
  gender and, 252
  kindergartner, case study of, 262–265
  learning disabilities, 254–255
    case study of ADD student with, 267–271
  medical management of, 256–257
  modifying instruction for students, 258–259
  organizing classroom for ADD students students, 257–258
  parallel behavior management programs, 260–261
  secondary student, case study of, 271–275
  second grader, case study of, 265–267
  secret signals for students with, 259

ADD students *continued*
  treatability of, 253–254
  treatments for, 255–261
Adler, Alfred, 135
After-school detention, 200–201
Aggressive behavior. *See also*
    Hitting
  of ADD students, 263
  time-outs for, 218
Anarchy, 29–30
Anger
  cooldown procedure, 122–125
  in permissive dance in
    classroom, 74
  in punitive dance in classroom,
    80–81
Antagonistic behavior, time-outs
    for, 217–218
Arguing, 103–104
  cut-off technique, 119–122
  logical consequences
    for, 192
Attention Deficit Disorder. *See*
    ADD students
Attention Deficit Hyperactivity
    Disorder (ADHD). *See* ADD
    students
Attention-seeking behavior, time-
    outs for, 215
Autocratic approach. *See* Punitive
    approach

B

Back-to-school nights, 21–22
Bargaining, 102–103
  with limited choices, 155
Behavior modification for ADD
    students students, 259–261
Biting, 213
Bribes, 105–106
Brief consequences, 171

Buddy helpers for ADD
    students, 258
Buddy teachers
  escorts to, 221
  for time-outs, 210
Burnout, 4

C

Cajoling, 104
Caring, firm limits and, 7
Check-in procedures, 117–119
  for ADD students, 260
  for arguing, 120
  diagram of, 118
  with limited choices, 155–156
Choices. *See also* Limited choices
  encouraging better choices,
    135–137
  exploring choices, 158–161
Classroom dance
  cooldown procedure, 122–125
  homework and, 224–226
  mixed dance in classroom,
    85–91
  permissive dance, 72–77
  punitive dance in classroom,
    77–84
  stopping, 116
Classroom management, 4
Clean slate, 173
  after off-campus suspension,
    201–202
  after time-out, 213
Commendations as encourage-
    ment, 142
Communication
  cooldown procedure,
    122–125
  Friday work folders, 16
Compliant children, 35
  testing limits by, 57

Concrete learning, 54–56
Conferences. *See* Teacher-parent
conferences
Conflicts, pattern of, 72
Consequences. *See also* Immediacy
of consequences; Logical
consequences; Natural
consequences; Time-outs
beginning and ending
of, 172
clean slates, 173
consistency of, 169–170
duration of, 171–172
effectiveness of, 166–173
firm limits, specifying
consequences in, 111
homework, failure to do,
239–240
importance of, 164–166
relatedness of, 170
respect and, 172–173
in retraining period, 173–175
testing and, 173–174
using consequences, 165–176
Consistency
of consequences, 169–170
of logical consequences, 202
office and classroom, consistency between, 160
Cooldown procedure, 122–125
for ADD students, 260
for quick-tempered teacher,
123–125
Cooperation
encouraging cooperation,
138–139
encouraging messages and,
133–135
logical consequences for
lack of, 191
Costly logical consequences,
193–202

Counselor, exploring choices
with, 160–161
Cut-off technique, 84, 119–122
for quick-tempered
teacher, 124
Cylert, 257

D

Daily behavior report cards, 79
Dances. *See* Classroom dances
Dawdling. *See* Procrastination
Debating, 103–104
Defiant behavior, time-outs
for, 217
Democratic approach, 46–51.
See also Firm limits
consequences, 167
diagram of, 49
message taught by, 50–51
Destructive acts, logical
consequences for, 191
Detention
after-school detention,
200–201
on-campus suspensions (OCS),
197–199
Saturday school, 199–200
Dexedrine, 257
Diagram
of check-in procedure, 119
of democratic interaction, 49
of mixed interaction, 45
of permissive dance, 73
of permissive interaction,
32–34
of punitive dance in classroom,
80–81
of punitive interaction, 40
for quick-tempered
teacher, 124
Direct messages, 110–111

283